SMILES MADE HERE

In *Smiles Made Here*, Dr. Sturgill provides invaluable insights for both orthodontic professionals and patients seeking the best care. This book brilliantly highlights the significance of a strong and positive culture in an orthodontic practice, ensuring an enjoyable experience for everyone involved. Whether you're a fellow practitioner striving to transform your practice or a parent seeking the ideal care for your child, this book is your guide to excellence.

—DUSTIN S. BURLESON, DDS, MBA

I have enjoyed educating, mentoring, and developing a life-long relationship with Dr. Jeremiah Sturgill over the past fifteen years. He is an extremely talented clinician with exceptional people skills. I am unbelievably proud of the highly skilled orthodontist and practice owner he has become. It is my privilege and honor to recommend this book to all colleagues in orthodontics.

—JAE H. PARK, DMD, MSD, MS, PHD
President, American Board of Orthodontics

T0203172

SMILES MADE HERE

DR. JEREMIAH STURGILL

SMILES MADE HERE

HOW CULTURE FORGES SUCCESS IN AN ORTHODONTIC PRACTICE

Advantage | Books

Published by Advantage Books, Charleston, South Carolina.
An imprint of Advantage Media.

ADVANTAGE is a registered trademark, and the Advantage colophon is a trademark of Advantage Media Group, Inc.

Printed in the United States of America.

10 9 8 7 6 5 4 3 2 1

ISBN: 978-1-64225-792-2 (Paperback)
ISBN: 978-1-64225-791-5 (eBook)

Library of Congress Control Number: 2024904142

Cover design by Analisa Smith.
Layout design by Matthew Morse.

This publication is designed to provide accurate and authoritative information in regard to the subject matter covered. It is sold with the understanding that the publisher is not engaged in rendering legal, accounting, or other professional services. If legal advice or other expert assistance is required, the services of a competent professional person should be sought.

Advantage Books is an imprint of Advantage Media Group. Advantage Media helps busy entrepreneurs, CEOs, and leaders write and publish a book to grow their business and become the authority in their field. Advantage authors comprise an exclusive community of industry professionals, idea-makers, and thought leaders. For more information go to **advantagemedia.com**.

To Pelegren, Theodore, and Sebastian—
may your sense of wonder draw you near to God

Contents

PART ONE

LEADING WITH CULTURE

PART TWO

CULTURE AND THE PATIENT EXPERIENCE

About the Author

DR. JEREMIAH STURGILL'S UNLIKELY STORY began in the foothills of the Appalachian Mountains—not what you may expect when thinking of the makings of a doctor and a leading business culture expert. Jeremiah's grit, zany personality, and undeniable faith make for a man who has a deep emotional intelligence along with an unwavering sense of purpose. His skillset is highlighted with board-certification as an orthodontist and clinician, but he is uniquely known as a champion and curator of a world-class team culture. His brand of systems, team morale, and business leadership is sought after by other business leaders as they seek to replicate the contagious office culture at Sturgill Orthodontics. The skillsets he posits can launch any business to build a culture that transforms coworkers into family; patients into friends and advocates; work into precision craft with fun; tasks into team accountability; and the mundane into joyful purpose.

Acknowledgments

To my beautiful wife, Riley. I would not be the man I am without you. I am in awe of your unique beauty, intellect, and faith. I love that you anchor me to what matters most. You cause me to slow down and enjoy the small moments with God, family, and nature. Thank you for being by my side and never doubting me even at times when I was my own biggest skeptic. May our love continue to grow.

To my children, Pele, Theo, and Sebi. Being greeted by your contagious smiles and giggles is the highlight of my day. My love for you is and always will be unconditional. I pray you would go through life impacting those around you, drawing others toward Christ. May you go beyond what you imagine.

To my mom and dad. You have never stopped speaking words of encouragement over me. I believed in what I could achieve only after you believed it first. I learned what is unteachable in academia from you both—the love for others through unrestrained generosity and the skills to build relationships. I know I am only where I am as I'm able to stand on the shoulders of generations of grueling hard work accompanied by deep love and commitment to family.

To my nanny. You were the most joyful, kind, and generous human I have ever known. Your unfailing love and unwavering faith in God impacted not only your family but an entire community. Your grit to not only survive but to thrive in the face of any adversity was a gift.

To my amazing team, Drs. Storie, Williams, and Harper. I could not be who I am today without each one of you. I learn from each of you the dedication you have not only to our work, our patients, and our community, but your commitment to your own families. I am grateful to work alongside so many women who show up every day with a posture of excellence toward their careers while balancing being mothers and wives. Seeing their dedication towards family even after a long day is inspiring to me; a reminder that I need to be at my best because I am humbled to lead a group of fierce women.

To my personal savior, Jesus Christ. I know everything I am is because of His goodness. I am so grateful and humbled that He bestowed upon me unique talents and gifts I can use for good. I am thankful for the valleys that cause my full dependence on His grace. To be successful as a professional, a business owner, even a father or husband is all for naught if I lose sight of my relationship with Christ. I pray to be an advocate for the faith in Christ and to always have a heart deeply seated in gratefulness and reliance on Him.

Introduction

THE IMPETUS FOR THE SUCCESS that Sturgill Orthodontics has experienced today really all started back when I was young. I hail from Big Stone Gap, Virginia, a very small town in the rural southwestern part of the state at the foothills of the Appalachian Mountains. It's an economically depressed area that doesn't have the educational resources of larger cities, but family values are very important here. That's really where I developed the ethos of Sturgill Orthodontics today.

You might be wondering what the ethos has to do with crafting smiles. At my practice, Sturgill Orthodontics, it's behind everything we do. Because of our belief in always putting ourselves in the patient's shoes, we've created a practice that others want to model their own orthodontic practices after.

Both of my parents were from the same area, and while they never had the opportunity for formal education, they were still successful in their own careers because of their innate work ethic and ability to overcome obstacles.

With an upbringing so rooted in family values, naturally my maternal grandmother, Nanny, had a big influence on me. Since both of my parents worked, she often looked after me. She was an amazingly hard worker herself; she worked in the school cafeteria, and when she knew one of the kids in line didn't have a lot of food at home, she would heap their plate. That made a big difference in a lot of people's lives. She never had a lot materially speaking, but she was always unbelievably cheerful, and she spread happiness wherever she went. She also believed that with God, anything is possible; she often told me: "You can do anything you want, the good Lord willing."

My father also used to make me see that there were bigger possibilities beyond the "snow globe world" we grew up in. My mother taught me the value of emotional intelligence and unbridled generosity. My parents were both fond of travel, and they wanted my sister and me to know that our success might not necessarily be found in our hometown, so I knew I'd have to look elsewhere to achieve the career I dreamed of. Ultimately, my wife and I went out and sought the best and, after eleven years, we brought all that knowledge and newly acquired connections back to our hometown region to serve the people here.

Since both my parents knew what it meant to grow up poor and not have access to higher education, they were determined that it would be different for me and my sister. They wanted to ensure that we would have the opportunity to go to college and learn to make money using our brains, not our backs.

After high school, I went to King University, a private Christian school, where I double majored in cell and molecular biology and business administration, the latter because I knew even then that I wanted to own my own business. Scholarships helped pay my way through college, supplemented by a stint as a Realtor—I had obtained my real estate license when I turned eighteen because I figured that was the most efficient way to make money with my schedule. Between organic chemistry classes and lab, for instance, I would go show a house. For dental school, however, I took out full loans.

I met my wife, Riley, while we were in college. We married after graduation and then moved to Arizona where we both went to dental school. After I finished my residency there, we moved back to Virginia, where Riley completed her residency in endodontics in Richmond while I worked as an associate there. We moved back because we were both planning to have our own practices one day, and, as professional services business owners (she now has her own endodontics practice nearby), we wanted our children to have life-shaping opportunities influenced by their grandparents and other family members.

Then, on January 1, 2016, I bought the practice that is now Sturgill Orthodontics. It was five hours away in Johnson City, Tennessee, which is nearer to both of our hometowns. I had decided to reach out to the orthodontist who had treated me as a kid to see if he might be interested in selling his practice—he was! In fact, he was actually so close to retirement that he had already had his practice appraised.

For eighteen months, while Riley stayed in Richmond to complete her residency, I'd drive back and forth from Johnson City on weekends to be with her. During those five-hour drives, I began working through ideas about how I wanted to revamp the practice that I had bought. Even though I was buying an existing practice, I knew what the ideal practice looked like in my mind: it was the best facility and had a highly skilled team with an unrivaled culture. When I shared some of my ideas with my colleagues, they would tell me that I really didn't need to go all out, as there wouldn't be that much competition since it was a rural area. But I thought, *Why doesn't our hometown deserve the best? What kind of person would I be if my goal is to just be 1 percent better?* My goal was to be the best—no questions asked.

On my first weekend drive to show up as the official new owner of the practice, amid all that planning in my head, I landed on the dreaded financials. Back then, the figures didn't add up: zero in the bank account with payroll, bills, and student loan payments in the hundreds of thousands of dollars coming due in a matter of weeks. I was filled with an unbelievable amount of stress and anxiety; I kept imagining myself showing up the first day at my newly purchased practice, meeting the team, and having them think to themselves, *"This guy's our new boss? I'm outta here."* I felt that they would think I was going to drive the practice straight into the ground; a big dumpster fire. Thankfully that's when the senior doctor from whom I bought the practice patted me on the shoulder and said, "It's going to be OK; you'll do great." He was a gentle encourager, and just like any practice owner who takes care of a practice for twenty years, it was like his child. But he graciously handed it over to me and continually encouraged me and told me that he knew it was in good hands.

That's when I realized that one of the most valuable assets I had was my team. I had a team that was already in place, and I needed to make sure they were on board with who I was and where I was going. I really needed them to see my vision and want to be a part of it. If they bought in, then it was no longer me alone trying to succeed but an entire team. No matter the changes and challenges that the practice would face during the transition—and hopefully the future growth of the practice—I was going to make sure that they were well taken care of. I needed a clear understanding of what my goals were so that I could convey to them where we were headed and why it was advantageous for them, for our patients, and for our community as a whole. Ultimately, no one left because of the transition. Even with a wall full of degrees, I still find that I don't always have all the answers, but I'm quick to recognize those weaknesses and surround myself with team members who are strong in those areas.

When daydreaming about what a world-class practice would look like, I felt like I was constantly faced with a decision tree of either continuing to play it safe and go with the status quo, or just going all in. I chose to go all in and revamp the physical appearance, the systems that were in place, and most importantly, the office culture—culture would be the key to creating the practice I envisioned. If we had an amazing culture, it would be a practice that patients wanted to come to, and then everything else would fall into place.

I never wanted to build a practice using billboards or coupons, although I know those work for some people. Too often I see orthodontists—or really any business—throw a lot of money into Google ads, or billboards, or direct mailers with the goal of bringing in patients or customers. But the reality is that they are not ready to receive patients because they haven't built a culture that welcomes people or the systems to onboard new patients or clients. They spend a lot of money just to get the phone to ring, then patients show up, and they still don't start treatment because the practice is not delivering what the patient was expecting or what they wanted. It's backward.

Instead, I wanted a practice known for providing world-class treatment because it was staffed by a team that was happy to show up every day and truly valued the patient experience. I was determined that the way we would market the practice would be word of mouth because of our world-class culture. My approach was to get the culture right and then put money into a website and search engine optimization (SEO) to bring in more patients. Today, I am confident that if someone calls my office, because of the team and protocols we have in place, that conversation is handled with the grace and confidence of booking a room at the Ritz Carlton.

Fast-forward seven years, and we have built the practice I dreamt of on those long drives. It's a state-of-the-art facility that would rival any practice in the country—one where culture drips off of every team member as they engage the community. Our conversion rate—or having a patient decide to start treatment—is in the mid- to high 80 percentile in an industry where standard is 70–75 percent. And in the few years since I took over the practice in 2016, we've gone from three hundred to twelve hundred starts per year. But even with that level of success, I still had that fear-of-failure feeling that I had on day one of buying the practice—I was still waiting on the other shoe to drop. Then a friend, who is an elder in our church, told me: "Why not you?" Even with all the visioning and planning and drive for excellence, I always thought someone else would be a better clinician, would have the preeminent culture, or would outperform our practice. But God gave me these talents and put me in a position to not only serve and lead my team but others in our profession—whether it's a consultation with a patient or a friend wanting some advice—which should give me some confidence because, after all, *why can't it be me who has the right answer?*

Still, I know that our success stems directly from patients knowing the minute they walk in—and every minute thereafter—that we're genuinely thankful they've chosen us for treatment; I take that seriously and so does my entire team.

In the chapters ahead, I'm going to share stories and tips about how we arrived at this place. I've written this book for two audiences: peers who would like their practice to mirror Sturgill Orthodontics and may be interested in coming in for a visit to see how it's done and patients or the parents of patients who are looking for a place to bring their child and want to know that they've made a good choice. Whether you're a practicing professional struggling to turn your ship around, taking over a practice and are anxious and want to the know the best way to spend your energy creating a good culture, or maybe someone who is doing a lot of research on what to look for in an orthodontist for your child or yourself, then this book is for you. Because a good culture is something that makes for an enjoyable experience for everyone.

PART ONE

Leading with Culture

WELCOME TO A PRACTICE BUILT ON CULTURE.
In this part of the book, I share how a successful practice operates and elements of a practice form the leadership perspective; basically, what a leader needs to know to create a successful culture. For peers reading this book, I'm sharing information and ideas to help evolve your practice into one with the ideal culture. At the end of each chapter, I've included a summary of takeaways from the chapter, titled "Practice Makes Perfect." For parents of patients or adult patients, each chapter contains a box titled "The Parents' Corner" with specific insights just for you on how to identify a culturally focused practice and why it's the best choice for your treatment.

CHAPTER ONE

It Takes a Team

FOR MOST PEOPLE, a trip to the orthodontist is not really a favorite part of the day. They're taking time out of their busy schedule to put themselves in a vulnerable position at the hands of people they don't really know all that well. I mean, if we really stop to think about it, it's crazy. We walk into an office of strangers and allow them to insert sharp metal objects into our mouth and poke around a little to examine the inside of our body. Then we pay for said torture!

But that's the very reason we built Sturgill Orthodontics to be a different kind of practice. When patients walk through the door at our practice, they're pleasantly surprised. Why? Because it's a place where *everyone* is happy and smiling and where everyone really works together as a team. It's clear from the minute you walk through the door that something really amazing is happening here. That's because of the culture we've built within.

We've made such a concerted effort to have a practice where people *want* to be that, time and again, patients and parents and other orthodontists have taken notice. It's not uncommon to hear words and phrases like, "Felt like I walked into an office in New York," or "How is it possible every person here is happy?" or "I've never been to another office like this," to describe the Sturgill team and the practice itself.

I recently found out it's extremely rare to have an office like ours. Many doctors whom I know and respect have told me they want a practice that operates like ours, but it's not what they have now. They want their office to have the same friendly, welcoming, warm culture and a staff that is genuinely happy to help one another out—working as an actual team.

I wrote this book to help you see how our practice became and maintains what it is today and why and how that's so important to patient care. It all starts first thing in the morning.

The Morning Huddle—More Than Just a Daily Meeting

At Sturgill Orthodontics, we start with a morning huddle. Now, that's not a new concept, of course. But there are a number of differences to our huddle.

For starters, there is the universal authenticity to how our team cares for one another and for patients. Even at 7:45 a.m., when we're having our morning huddle, there's an almost pulsating energy in the room from a team that is excited to tackle the day ahead—together. There's a sense of warmth and camaraderie, and people who witness it feel it right away. Whether it's a new team member or a visiting peer, they're met with a warm and friendly greeting from smiling team members who are genuinely happy, introduce themselves, and welcome the newcomer onboard. At other practices, I've been told, newcomers are not introduced right away, and there are no morning huddles; often newcomers are met with an awkward silence, and instead of a morning huddle, everyone just takes their station and starts working. Or if there is a morning huddle, it's nothing like ours, which has a few specific purposes. Let me tell you about them.

To understand what we're out to conquer that day. Like any kind of group, whether it's a sports team or a church mission group, our huddle is about understanding our goals. We're starting the day off together, so we need to figure out what is ahead of us and how to conquer it together.

To bond the team. The morning huddle is a great time to just make sure that everyone feels included, that no one is left out. That's important to do every day because, as a team grows, there is a natural tendency for it to segregate and for people to become more independent, more siloed. In any practice, there may be people in administration, in finance, at the front desk, and in clinical roles, and the only time they may really interact with coworkers is in that morning meeting. So, we think it's crucial to bond at the start of the day in order to continue to feel like a team—every day.

To take the pulse of the team. In the huddle, we go around the group one-by-one to allow everyone to weigh in on the day's activities. It's a short meeting, only fifteen to twenty minutes, so it's typically just a rapid fire from everyone that has something to share. The majority of the time these weigh-ins are about the daily schedule or operational, administrative, or clinical announcements about something other members of the team need to know.

However, this open forum is also an opportunity for the team to share what's going on in their personal lives. Letting people share some of their personal wins or concerns helps us keep a pulse on the team. We really want to know when someone has really good or bad news to share—they adopted a new pet, bought a new home, their child is sick, or they just found out a beloved family member is terminally ill. When it's good news, it gives us all something to celebrate. When it's heavy news, it lets us know that we need to give that person a little extra encouragement or lift that day—they might really be struggling after a sleepless night. That also lets me know that, as a leader, I need to check in on that person and give them a little extra grace that day.

It is uplifting when someone is surrounded by a team that really cares. When they allow themselves to be a little vulnerable, then other members of the team can often bring new perspective and lighten the load for someone carrying an extra burden. It's not uncommon for tears to be shed in a morning huddle. Having that type of vulnerability is what allows our team to have authentic relationships with one another. But we're also a place where humor is welcome, and often awkwardly inserted by yours truly, as a way to balance out the serious stuff, like the business of clinical care. I have a pretty zany sense of humor, so it's not uncommon for the huddle to leave the team laughing and really energized—sometimes a real feat at 7:30 a.m. when people might be a little tired, or slow-starting, or their mind is in a different place.

To deliver inspiration and gratitude. At the end of the huddle, one of the doctors shares something inspirational, a quote or a Bible verse designed to help the team throughout the day, followed by one of the doctors praying for our team and our patients that day. Then we spend a couple of minutes sharing notes from our gratitude journals, which we ask every member of the team to maintain as a way of helping them see all there is to be thankful for.

Coaching for the Huddle

As I mentioned, the morning huddle that we do is nothing new: many practices do one, but often either they have little substance and leave people with a "why bother" attitude or they are very serious briefings, often led by the practice leader or a team lead.

I wanted the Sturgill Orthodontics huddle to be worth showing up for, so over time, I've helped coach the team to understand what the meeting is for—and what it's not for. At our morning huddles, no one person does all the talking. In my experience, when that's what a morning huddle involves, the members of the team often don't get much out of the meeting. It's also important that it not be a lamenting session that drags the team down with irrelevant, negative news: "we used to do it that way but no one liked it," or "today is going to be so hard and it's raining," or just a lot of *waah waah* that really helps no one.

Important points need to be relevant and addressed very quickly. For instance, clinical information won't mean much to the financial team and vice versa, so those items need to be covered at a high level. But the operations manager may need the entire team to know something relevant, so she needs to be heard and in a way that makes it clear that the material is important. For instance, there's no sitting down to share the news that we need five more patients to start treatment that day in order to meet our monthly goals. That news needs a certain kind of energy—it needs to be delivered standing up and with a sense of authority—subtle but important differences.

Here's an example of how our morning huddle has a different kind of energy: when I coached our operations manager, Holly, on her approach, telling her that her presentation needed a little more oomph, she said, "You want excitement? I'll give you excitement"—

and she did. At the next morning's huddle, another member of the team pulled a giant Santa-like bag into the room, and out jumped Holly to announce we had hit our goal. That's the kind of culture we have—it's one where people are not afraid to be a little ridiculous or even jokingly give me a hard time.

It's about Balance

Having a little fun can be a difficult concept for a dental professional who spent years going to a dental school and expects to be taken as a serious professional. But it's OK to have fun sometimes; displaying a little humor doesn't mean there is an equal decrease in professionalism or in the quality or seriousness of the work. There should be a balance between having fun and being professional, especially when it comes to the clinical side of the practice—that's where we draw the line at Sturgill Orthodontics.

When it comes to treatment of patients, we have created certain protocols and procedures, and we expect them to be followed every day—with no deviation. That's not to say we won't listen to an idea for improvement; the doctors will research the viability of such suggestions, and, if we all agree, we'll make the change universal. We also know that solutions need to be tailored to patient needs, but again, there are protocols in place that help us know what treatment we need to do when. That level of seriousness on the clinical side is one reason we like to have a little fun throughout the day.

Check Eeyore at the Door

As a leader, the practice doctor sets the tone and the energy of the office. It's up to you to raise the bar and then inspire your team to reach that bar. I'm a pretty outgoing person, but knowing that it's up to me to set the bar is a challenge that even I have to rise to every day. Like anyone, there are things in my life that keep me awake at night—currently, I have very young children, for instance. But even after a night of little sleep, I know I can't come grumping and slumping into the office and set that tone for the day; I call it "checking Eeyore at the door." There will always be outlier days, but by and large, your team needs to know that you're there for them because they're going to mimic and mirror your energy level and your enthusiasm. If you're coming to work with low energy, or with a bland attitude, or just trying to make it through the day, your team will notice, and it will set the tone for the entire practice. And I expect my team to do the same because when we're at the office, we're there to perform well.

You can have fun and still be a great doctor. People will still take you seriously even if you build a practice that is a happy and fun place to be. In fact, people will actually trust you more if they feel that they're getting the real you and that you're not putting on a show.

That's different from an ego-led practice, one where the doctor has an air of superiority over everyone else. One of our treatment coordinators calls it "doctor syndrome," when the doctor leader of a practice has the attitude that they are better than everyone else, and they talk down to people—the team and the patients.

A truly successful practice doesn't revolve around one person; it takes a team to perform all that needs to be done to meet each patient's needs. The team has a big impact on the success of the practice, and they must touch patients in a positive way. But when a practice revolves around a leader's ego, the team ends up being anxious about making the doctor happy, and the patients' needs come second—that can cripple a practice because the team feels like, no matter what they do, they're going to be wrong. The result is a very dissatisfied, very unhappy team. They're filled with angst because they're always afraid they'll make the doctor mad or the patient mad, or both. No one is ever happy.

At Sturgill Orthodontics, our mission is to "make someone's day," and we do that by crafting smiles in the physical and nonphysical sense. In other words, we use our expertise and technology to physically create great smiles, and we also like to do things that make our patients show their smiles. I don't want my team's decision tree to be about what makes me happy but to be about doing whatever is best for the patient in any situation. It's a more harmonious decision tree. If they make the patient happy, then the doctors in the practice are happy too. When a patient is thrilled and the team member is being cheered on for doing a good job, they're better equipped to make good decisions.

You Can't Do It Alone

As the doctor leading the practice, you're the trained and experienced professional. But you can't do it alone. When you have a great team that works together like a well-oiled machine, it's so much easier to handle unforeseen variables.

Too often, leaders view the members of their team as being disposable; if one doesn't work out, then they'll just replace that person with someone else next week. What these leaders don't realize is that disposing of a team member also disposes of their abilities and any training that they were given. A leader should never hire with the mindset that a team member is disposable. Instead, you should be putting so much time and energy into training the members of your team that you're heartbroken that they would be leaving. The main reason for attrition should be because that person's life situation changes: they move or decide to stay home with young children. If you're hiring a good fit for the team, then they should not be leaving because they did not enjoy the culture or they found a "better opportunity." And the only reason you should be letting someone go is because they are not a good fit and they are harming the culture.

It's all about grooming and pruning your culture to ensure you don't end up with people who stir up gossip and attitude to the point that you end up with an office that's about to fall apart.

When you think about it, creating a team with a great culture—one that puts the patient first—is a little like producing a fine glass of wine with all its nuances and notes. When you get a sip of our practice, it's a complex but pleasant experience. It's a place with a very refined, very polished clinical side that unexpectedly but delightfully blends with just the right amount of humor to make for an enjoyable visit.

Some of the best wines, of course, come from vines with deep and complex roots—plants that didn't start out with the easiest growing environment but kept seeking the best nutrients and atmosphere in which to thrive. For us, creating that ideal environment starts with hiring; we want to make sure we're growing only the best grapes and pruning out those that can ruin the vineyard. Then we work every day to cultivate the culture of the practice so that it is a place that makes people feel they can take root.

And just like a celebrated vintage isn't produced by a single hand, it takes a team to create our winning environment. Everyone has a hand in ensuring what is a complex biological process be a smooth experience.

The Parents' Corner

A Sense of "Wow"

As a parent, you may not be aware of the offices that have spent thousands of hours to create systems that make your appointment flow easily. However, you surely remember the experiences you've had at offices when you could tell that team members didn't know how to work efficiently with one another.

Our goal is for you to come and go from our office with a sense of "Wow, that was so effortless." That's only possible with a team that looks through every single patient appointment for that day and considers any possible complications with the schedule, any possible issues, and how we can overcome them before they actually become a problem. For example, if you show up and need a mouthguard the next day, in our morning huddle, we discuss how we'll make that happen even though the lab tech happens to be on vacation that week. That all goes off without a hiccup because we start every day trying to problem-solve issues so that our patients have a seamless experience.

A State-of-the-Art Facility

Part of having a great working environment comes down to having great systems in place, such as the best technology, processes, and a state-of-the-art facility.

When I purchased the practice that now bears my name, it was definitely a well-functioning operation. It came with a good team that, for the most part, worked well together. But it wasn't an *environment* that reflected my personality. I've always believed that, if you're going to be somewhere most of your day, you should enjoy that space. If you don't enjoy it, then why would your team enjoy it? To me, it's always seemed odd to find a disconnect between a doctor's office and home aesthetics: the doctor's office may be unkempt, unclean, and look like it hasn't been updated since 1975 while their home is spotless, modern, and everything works. For me and my wife, Riley, our situation is somewhat the opposite—we each have clean and modern offices (hers is a separate practice), but with three young children at home, needless to say our house is not spotless. However, since we spend the majority of our waking hours in our practices, we believe they should look and operate at their best because that's what makes our family life successful.

I find it frustrating when doctors don't invest in their practices. An office doesn't need to be an architectural wonder of marble and mahogany, but it should have good lighting and be clean and organized. There should be enough space for team members to work without stumbling over one another. Both patients and team should feel comfortable there—simple things.

Then there's the equipment. Some doctors will spend hours tinkering with a $5,000 piece of equipment to try to save the $200 maintenance call, when all it would take is starting one more patient to purchase a replacement. You and your team are going to be frustrated if you don't have properly working equipment and a nice facility, so think about the decisions you're making from an efficiency perspective. Your time as the doctor needs to be patient-focused, not constantly problem-solving on dated computers or squeaky printers. If you can buy a brand-new piece of equipment and it means that you're able to see more patients because of it, you've actually made money instead of wasting it spending time tinkering with a piece of equipment that just needs to be replaced. With that reframed mindset, it becomes clear what to do when a piece of equipment breaks.

Open Your Mind with Boredom

It's hard to be aware of what's broken in your office if you don't take the time to sit and reflect on what you and your team are spending time constantly fixing. You'll never be able to discover the bottleneck if you're living in the bottleneck.

Pausing for a few minutes to think through a problem is often the best way to solve it. But finding those few minutes can be a challenge if you're in the mode of improving or building out your practice. Yet according to podcaster Manoush Zomorodi, author of *Bored and Brilliant: How Spacing Out Can Unlock Your Most Productive and Creative Self*, letting your mind daydream or wander ignites what is known as your brain's "default mode," a term coined by neuroscientist Marcus Raichle. In essence, being in default mode originally meant the brain was "at rest," but as it turns out, when the brain is supposedly "switched off," it's actually making new connections and forming new ideas because it's able to access the subconscious.[1] In other words, taking a little time to indulge in boredom and letting your mind relax can actually help you solve problems. Start by purposefully losing your cell phone.

When my wife and I were working in different cities—she was in Richmond finishing her residency and I was in Johnson City working in the practice I had just bought—I used to take that five-hour drive to spend weekends with her. In truth, a lot of the planning for the way

---

1   Manoush Zomorodi, "How boredom can lead to your most brilliant ideas," Ted Talk, accessed April 10, 2021, https://www.ted.com/talks/manoush_zomorodi_how_boredom_can_lead_to_your_most_brilliant_ideas/transcript?language=en.

Sturgill Orthodontics works today was done during those meditative road trips on that long, straight drive.

As the leader of the practice, you need to take the time to let your mind wander through your office. Just take time alone to look at your practice through a different, daydreaming lens: How can you improve processes? How can you improve customer satisfaction? How can you better serve your team? Who on your team is quietly making a huge impact and thriving? Who on your team needs coaching? Should new products or procedures be considered? How are you leading well, and where are your blind sides? Who will tell you the truth about your leadership? Chances are, you'll discover some amazing ways to make a big difference.

Orthodontics is no different from any other business, in that there is a myriad of cogs and levers that we must continually try to tweak and adjust to make sure that everything is humming at peak performance. So many people think that their business should operate on autopilot, but that ultimately just means letting it coast to its own death. So, you must constantly look for ways to improve systems and raise the bar. But that should be done in a way that always allows the team to continually put forth an attitude that is real and authentic—in the next chapter, we'll look at what that means.

Practice Makes Perfect

- As the practice leader, it's up to you to create change. If there's something that you don't like or that you want changed, you have the responsibility to make that happen, not only for yourself but also for the other members of the team.

- Your team looks to you for guidance; never forget that you set the tone.

- People spend a lot of time at work, so why not make it a place that everyone enjoys.

- Make sure that the team members that you bring on are good fruit and that you are quick to prune away anyone who threatens to destroy the vine.

- Continually cultivate and fertilize your existing team. Don't be so focused on your new people that you forget the person who has been loyal to the practice for years.

- Make sure that there is a universal understanding that, every day, you start as a team and you finish as a team. There's no room for "not my job" in a practice built on culture.

- A practice led by an authoritarian is a practice built on fear, which will cripple the team's ability to serve patients.

CHAPTER TWO

An Authentic Workplace

MOST OFFICES HAVE STATEMENTS to help guide the team for how things are done. A mission statement, a vision statement, a values statement—a few sentences or paragraphs that attempt to encompass all of the core competencies that people who work for the company will ideally have or beliefs that they will ideally follow.

We have those at Sturgill Orthodontics. But we also have something more—our team agreement—ten bullet points that are easy to read and understand. They are displayed on a plaque next to the time clock so that everyone can at least subconsciously glance at them as they clock in and out each working day. At the annual meeting every year, we have everyone write down the ten team agreements—from memory—with prizes for team members who have them down word for word. Our team agreement has ten points and they are not all uniquely original; many of them came from other sources that I researched after taking over the practice. What makes them easy to memorize is that they are so authentic—they really are core to our culture. They are actions that our team members actually live. Here are the ten measures that we all agree to follow every day.

1. *I agree to CHOOSE a positive attitude.* What this one is saying is that we're a glass-half-full kind of group. We *choose* every day to see things from the positive point of view.

2. *I agree to open and honest communication.* This one is a real key to the success of our culture. Especially as the practice has grown, we've found it crucial to have open and honest communication. One reason for this is because we want experienced team members to help new team members learn the very specific procedures and protocols at the practice; if they see a new person incorrectly performing a procedure, they're to show them how to do it correctly. But if the experienced team member instead just corrects the new person's mistake without telling them, then over time, the experienced team member will grow frustrated for taking on so much extra work, and the new team member will never improve. Problems don't spontaneously correct themselves, and it's more embarrassing and awkward to wait six months to address a problem than to just say something right away. Even though it can seem awkward to correct someone—partly for fear of hurting their feelings—we've found that it actually makes new team members feel respected and more like part of the team.

3. *I agree to PTS (Patient > Team > Self).* This is about making our priorities our patients, then the team, and then ourselves, in this order.

4. *I agree to constant improvement.* This agreement is an acceptance of change and a continual reminder that Sturgill Orthodontics is a progressive practice; we're constantly looking for ways to improve.

5. *I agree to be efficient and effective with my time.* We want to have fun at work, but we also work hard. This agreement is about not dilly-dallying with tasks and being a good team player, working just as hard as coworkers so that no one is required to pick up slack.

6. *I agree to come to work "show" ready.* I took this concept from training I underwent at the Disney Institute. This is about showing up every day looking like a professional, which means different things for different members of the team. For some members of what is usually an all-female team in an orthodontics office, it may mean very little makeup; for others, it may mean looking like they just walked out of a salon. As one team member says, "Dress like you're going to brunch with your girlfriends." However it's defined, it means clean, unwrinkled scrubs and a fresh appearance; no one should be showing up disheveled and wearing wrinkled scrubs covered with dog fur and looking like they just rolled out of bed and forgot to brush their teeth and hair—that doesn't instill confidence in anyone's clinical capabilities. Naming the agreement "show" ready reduces the awkwardness that male practice leaders often struggle with when holding a conversation about appearance with female team members. When we explain this agreement to team members, we tell them "show" ready means however you presented yourself at your interview when you came in to seek a professional job with a medical provider—that's how we expect people to present themselves at work every day.

7. *I agree to coach my team and to be coached.* If the owner of a practice is the only coach of that practice, then they're limiting the rate of growth because there is not enough time to coach everyone well. But if team members are guided to coach one another, it's better for team-building. Coaching is an important part of the practice, so I talk more about it in chapter 4.

8. *I agree to build relationships with patients.* Patients are not just chart numbers, but they are people whom we want to get to know as well—after all, you never know when a patient lying back in the chair might just need someone to talk to on any given day. Agreeing to build relationships with patients ensures that team members don't spend their time talking over a patient's head to another team member; instead, they are focused on the patient in the chair and taking time to get to know them. That's especially important with, for instance, teenagers—we see so many who are bullied to the nth degree online because of their teeth. Being in the chair might be one of the few times that teen is away from parents, away from school, and with an adult that can give them some one-on-one attention, an adult who is a medical professional whom they trust. Team members know that it's OK to go long on an appointment if it's because they were taking extra time getting to know the patent.

9. *I agree to take ownership.* This one is huge. It is so easy for people to see a problem and then just ignore it or assume someone else will fix it—they just try to pass it on. For instance, if a computer monitor is not working, does the team member check to see whether it's plugged in or do they call the help desk—or do they just move to a different computer and leave the problem for someone else? At our practice, team

members take ownership of a problem until it is solved. And that's every team member and any problem; if someone from clinical notices that the coffeemaker is out of coffee, then that individual should start a new pot of coffee. In fact, we are always looking for problems to solve; when everyone has an eye out for them, it helps keep everything running smoothly instead of having to put out fires all day.

10. *I agree to do "whatever it takes."* Sometimes, a patient's treatment is really difficult, but that doesn't mean we're just going to give up on them or cut corners. We're going to do whatever it takes to deliver.

Within the first few weeks of joining Sturgill Orthodontics, almost every new team member says the same thing: "I can't believe how much everyone helps each other here." Other practices, they tell us, can be very territorial; they might have tried to assist someone with cleanup of a task, only to be asked, "What are you doing here? Did you think I needed your help? This is my chair; this is my job."

Here, it's about starting the day as a team and finishing the day as a team. For instance, if one team member, let's say Lisa, sees another team member, Teresa, working on a patient into the lunch hour, Lisa may ask Teresa if she needs assistance to finish up so that she can go to lunch too. It's the same when a team member needs to leave early to pick up a child or get to an appointment or even make it to a ballgame; it's not uncommon for someone else to step up and work late in their place. It's not always the same person leaving early or staying late either. When you see team members just helping one another without being asked, you know you have built a successful culture.

As we routinely tell interviewing candidates, this is not a place where anyone says, "That's not my job." Anyone making that statement here can consider that to be their last day. None of us is too good for any job. I'm not above taking out the trash if it will help my team. Although most of the time they take care of those kinds of tasks, sometimes it's on me to intentionally make that kind of effort so that they see I'm part of the team too—that I'm not above any task that needs to be done.

When we hire someone new, we want them to feel comfortable and welcome from day one; we don't want anyone to feel awkward or out of place. We start by sending them through a full-day orientation, which is as much about the culture of the office as it is about their role. Over time, we found that the orientation even needs to include small details that aren't necessarily written down, such as the fact that the snacks and sparkling waters in the employee breakroom are available to the team for free, or where the light switches and shred box are located, or that they are welcome to join team members who take their break outside when the weather is nice. It's easy to overlook small details when you've been part of the team for some time, but for someone who is brand new, having an experienced team member even over-explain the obvious can help a new person feel at ease and like a welcome part of the team.

New hires are required to sign a team agreement as part of orientation. We want them to know right away that we take the ten points very seriously. It's a great tool to have in each employee's file as a point of reference; if you use it to let a team member know when they are not really living one or more of the agreements, then you have documentation if it comes time to let someone go.

To consider content for a similar agreement for your practice, ask your team what they think some of the core competencies are in your practice. Ask them what they think is important—you may be surprised.

"Culture Eats Strategy for Breakfast"

Determining the core competencies in your practice is one way to determine culture in your practice, because with a great culture, you can overcome anything. Peter Drucker has said, "Culture eats strategy for breakfast." Our culture has allowed us to get through some rough days, tough patient cases, or just those moments when I stick my foot in my mouth—like when I welcome a new mom and her son to the practice (it's her daughter). With a great culture, my team is there to help us quickly recover.

No one can strategize for all the things that can happen in an office, but culture can help you overcome anything—even office drama.

People always think there's more drama in an office made up mostly of women, and as a male leader of a primarily female support staff, it can be a challenge to figure out how to deal with it appropriately. But if you ask some of the members of my team, they'll tell you there's no bigger drama than when a man is involved. Just ask any of the married members of the team about the last time they and their husband had a cold at the same time; while he's lying in bed, she's still running around doing laundry and taking care of the kids. Having often visited the worksite at my father's construction business, I saw how a group of men can be some of the most dramatic people around—just nail a two-by-four in the wrong place at a construction site and you'll see what I mean. They may not burst out in tears, but they'll sure let you know you messed up. It's a different kind of drama than in an office, but it's still drama.

Office drama seems to be more passive-aggressive. As a leader, you have to be more aware of the subtleties, especially the nonverbal cues. Those might be as simple as how one member of the team responds to another's morning greeting; one person might perceive (or misperceive) something a little off in the other's tone.

Instead of letting things simmer, we address them quickly. If the situation doesn't resolve, then we help that person find an opportunity elsewhere—a nice way of saying we let them go. It's never pleasant to have to turn out a team member, but it also helps your practice when everyone knows you don't put up with drama. When new team members come in, if they hear a story about someone's behavior that ended in their termination, they learn that there is a standard, and when that line gets crossed, they'll lose their job.

As a leader, it's your job to make sure this line in the sand is visible to all so that they know that, in the office, they must act like professionals. We tell candidates in their interview: never lie, steal, do anything that could intentionally harm a patient, or cause a lot of drama—or you will have to find another place to work.

When you draw that line, stick to it. If you're the kind of leader who hates confrontation and relies on your clinic or office manager to take care of problems, you'll come off as passive-aggressive yourself. A passive-aggressive leader who doesn't like confrontation can breed the same in the team culture. But it's not confrontation; it's communication. If you see a problem with a team member but don't address it when it happens, instead asking someone else to take care of the situation, you're making it harder for everyone. Not only is it hard for the manager—who likely didn't even witness the problem—but also for the team member who is now embarrassed because you didn't approach her directly. Clinical matters are especially important for the doctor to address with the team member—who better to explain a clinical procedure than the doctor?

Having seen this happen in other office settings—where the leader wanted the office manager to take care of a situation—I was determined to just handle matters directly at Sturgill Orthodontics. Initially, I thought I would be perceived as a jerk, but instead, I've had employee after employee come into my office and tell me how much they appreciate that I just talk to them directly.

The Parents' Corner
The Sniff Test for Authenticity

We routinely have parents come in for a second opinion and tell us that they are here because something just didn't smell right at the first practice they went to—and something about Sturgill Orthodontics feels just right. I feel like moms are especially good at this; they seem to have an extra sense that lets them know something isn't quite right. Kind of like the mom who always knows when their child is not telling the truth—they can just smell it.

Authenticity can be hard to really articulate, but you know when you feel it—or when you smell it, as some of our moms say. It's just a certain vibe, and you know it when you enter the practice.

At the end of the day, as humans, we're good at picking up little subtleties such as a person's eye contact, posture, and other little things; our mind is constantly calculating these to let us know whether a person is telling us the truth. That's how people who visit Sturgill Orthodontics know that, when we say, "Welcome, nice to see you," we mean it. When we say we're the best, we really believe it.

Being authentic with everyone—in or out of the office—helps build trust with the team and with patients. That comes from letting them see your heart.

Practice Makes Perfect

- Create your own team agreement, and make sure that you're living it out and that it's not just something on the wall.
- Don't make the team agreement something used randomly or presented to a new team member after two years. Make sure everyone knows that it is intentional from day one.
- When interviewing a candidate, ask yourself whether you feel at ease in the conversation. Do you trust the answers you're being given? If you don't feel the candidate is being authentic, then don't hire them. One team member I interviewed was so nervous that she giggled and apologized through the entire interview, but we loved her authenticity. Her nervousness showed that she really cared.
- Remind yourself of how much lighter and better you feel when you let someone know about an issue that has been bothering you. Your employees will feel the same if they are direct with their coworkers and don't keep secrets that fester.
- Hire the right people, and you will eliminate the drama.

CHAPTER THREE

Let Them See Your Heart

FAITH IS DEFINITELY PART of what defines our culture. It's not required for employment at Sturgill Orthodontics, but our team is very aware of our faith, and they know that our prayers go out to them when their times are challenging. We're never shy about it in front of patients either, and we let them know that our heart goes out to them when we find out they are going through tough times.

While we are faith-forward leaders, this is not what I would call a faith-branded practice. It's fine for some companies to be very deliberate about including faith in their branding, but we feel that's the wrong approach for us because it might make some patients uncomfortable. We want it to be crystal clear that everyone is welcome here, and we have patients from a wide variety of socioeconomic classes, races, genders, and faiths.

To ensure everyone on the team feels welcome in our environment, I let candidates know during their interview that I'm a Christian as are the other two doctors in the practice and that we make decisions based on our faith. Again, no one has to profess to be a Christian to work here, but we want them to be comfortable with the idea of prayer at work to give them the opportunity to self-select out before we offer them a job. When we pray at the morning meeting, our goal is to center the practice and remind everyone of why we're doing what we're doing—we want to do good work for our patients, and we want them to know that they are loved and cared for.

Faith helps guide me as a leader, and I feel it holds me to a higher standard. Others look to me as their example of what a Christian is—how to navigate difficult situations and react to anger, gracefully let someone go, and don't lie or manipulate business or patients. I feel all of those are constant examples of what it means to lead as a Christian who is forward with their faith. Basically, they're ways in which I show people my heart.

Showing Your Heart

Letting people see your heart can be a difficult concept for a lot of leaders in business because it's about making a personal connection. But it makes all the difference in creating an environment where the team feels they're with people who care. Then they, in turn, can feel comfortable, thus naturally showing that same sense of caring toward patients.

We really look at our team as family. It's a very professional, fast-paced, and efficient practice, but we also have fun and share our lives outside the office—weddings, baby showers, get-togethers. Being family means we also try to help one another when in need. If someone's car broke down, we find a way for them to borrow our car.

If they have to leave their house—maybe because of a divorce and no money for a down payment on an apartment—we find them a hotel for a couple of weeks. We even lend money, if needed, so that our team members don't have to go to a predatory lender. Sometimes, the need is just an open ear or a shoulder to help someone vent their frustrations or worries—whether related to work or personal life.

A personal touch means thinking about little extras that mean a lot to someone else. For instance, when we give a bonus, we want to do it in a way that makes the most impact on the person receiving it. That might mean giving them a cash bonus so that they can go buy something special for themselves instead of having that extra income show up on a paycheck where it goes into a bank account that is dedicated only to household or family expenses. When the money is accompanied by a handwritten note, it's even more special—to both the team member and to me. I find it very humbling to sit down and try to figure out what really matters to each team member. When considering their circumstances, what words of encouragement can I offer to make them feel appreciated and valued?

We also show heart to our patients by doing the right thing for them. For example, let's say a patient isn't following their treatment plan like they were supposed to and they end up needing an appliance that costs several hundred dollars to correct the situation. We just take care of that cost because we want to ensure the patient gets the desired outcome. Practices often get caught up in nickel-and-diming patients for treatment. But we feel like we charged the parent a cost for treatment, and we just need to get the job done.

When a child's teeth have shifted because their treatment was interrupted by something beyond their control, we just put braces and retainers back on them for free. We saw that several times during the pandemic—missionary families sent home from overseas had interrupted treatment. Even though, in many cases, the treatment we provide was actually a higher standard, we saw that as a blessing to have the opportunity to do something for someone giving their life in service somewhere else in the world to someone in need.

We also give free care to patients in our community who clearly have financial hardships, for example, when a primary caregiver is the child's grandmother who doesn't have insurance but sees the difference orthodontic treatment will make in the life of the child. (Grandmothers are my "kryptonite," my team says, because of my relationship with my own beloved "Nanny.") Most of the time, they don't tell us they can't afford treatment, so in order to avoid awkwardness, we have our treatment coordinators inform the parent that the treatment is free or significantly discounted. We never have the doctors in the practice share that information, often because the patient or parent cries upon hearing it, and we don't want them to feel embarrassed. In fact, sometimes the coordinators cry as well.

Sometimes, however, the parent may share that they really can't afford treatment, but since the child is being bullied because of their teeth, we know we have to figure out a way to make it work. It might be a single parent, or someone we know we really need to give a substantial discount.

At Sturgill Orthodontics, our staff sees that we're not continuously pausing treatment and asking *what is the best financial decision.* That's a value statement of how we practice; we look at every single case and decide what the case needs, how to get it done, and how to get it done well. Whatever is best for the patient, we just do it. It's painful when a patient comes to us from another practice and tells us how they feel trapped in their braces because they were behind on a payment or that maybe a deviation from treatment was not done because they had already paid and the treatment would cost extra. That's just not how we practice.

But even when treatment is free, the patient still gets the same level of care. And we don't do it to stroke egos. We don't give away hundreds of thousands of dollars of free treatment every year to make us look good. We do it because it's part of our culture.

Leading Chairside

What happens from the clinical perspective also tells a lot about the practice culture. Your team will see how the decisions you make affect patient treatment, and they will follow your lead. They'll know if you're going out of your way to help patients—they'll also know if you're cutting corners. For instance, if a patient has a problem that they don't see or understand with their untrained eye, do you, the provider, go through the effort to correct it or just let it go? If a patient is happy with their outcome, but their teeth don't quite fit together perfectly, which could ultimately lead to wear, do you, the provider, fix the problem knowing that the extended treatment time is out of your pocket, not the patient's?

For some reason, particularly in the field of healthcare, there seems to be a hierarchy. Yes, doctors go through more training and education than other members of the support team, so there is sometimes this aura that no one on the team knows patient care better than the doctor. In some cases, that may be true, but less education and training don't always equate to less intelligence or a greater ability to be deceived. In other words, just because doctors were educated and trained in a procedure doesn't mean they can shortcut patient care without a member of the support team noticing.

Doctors hire smart people to assist them in treatment, and in the orthodontist's office, those intelligent people are sitting chairside, right there next to the doctor—and next to the patient. Since they're so smart, they know what good treatment looks like. They see what you do as the provider with one patient, and what you do with the same needs on another patient, so they know when you're cutting corners. Plus, they may also have worked in another office and have seen what bad treatment looks like. So, while you may be able to convince the patient that what you're doing is best for them, the team member sitting chairside will know otherwise. They may not say anything because they don't want to risk losing their job, but they will know and they'll perceive that as being OK in your office.

Conversely, when you truly have the patient's best interests at heart, your team will see that too, and they'll follow your lead. I've seen my team kick into gear with me chairside when they know that I'm working on a difficult case. Sometimes this job can be physically demanding; it can be a little rough leaning over a patient for thirty minutes to address a challenge. But when the team knows that, yes, this is going to be tough, but it's got to be done because it's the right thing to do, they step right up. I've seen them do it chairside as well when they're working on a patient and realize that they've got a difficult task ahead. Because of our culture, they just step up to the task because they know it's the right thing to do.

We have team members who purposely joined our practice because they heard from other people that it was really hard work, but it was the best place to work. One clinical team member even told us how, when working at another practice, she would go home at night bothered by the procedures she had done that day. Even though the patient wouldn't be harmed by the treatment, it could have been so

LET THEM SEE YOUR HEART

much better if the doctor did not cut corners and think no one would know—but that team member certainly noticed.

When coming to a fork in the road where treatment is concerned, there can sometimes be the hard route versus the easy route, and if your team sees you choosing the hard route over the easy one because it's the right thing to do, then they will do the same when the time comes. If your team members believe in you and your practice, they will be your biggest advocates. Then they can look at a patient with 100 percent authenticity and say, "Yes, you've come to the right place. Trust me, there's nowhere where the doctors are going to work harder. We're not perfect, but we're going to give it all we've got." You can't fake that.

Generosity—A Word of Caution

In this chapter, I've shared how Sturgill Orthodontics has a very generous spirit. But there's such a thing as being too generous. That can produce a negative culture if the team takes advantage of the situation—if they come to expect overly special treatment.

I've seen this happen to the point that it almost ruined a practice culture and the doctor had to basically start over by taking the blame for the situation and then letting every member of the team go on a Friday and informing them that they could come back on Monday and interview for their position but in a practice with a new culture. It was a huge risk on the leader's part, but it worked, because everyone came back on Monday and the practice managed to reset. From then on, everyone knew that they were fortunate to be at a job with great benefits, but they could be fired if they took advantage of the situation.

I've never had to go to that extreme at Sturgill Orthodontics, but there was a point some time ago where it seemed that there was a lot of grumbling about things. While some of the longtime team members have always been super thankful for the benefits we provide—having been in the workplace longer, they know that it's not all about perks— newer members of the team had different expectations. At the time, I was putting out thousands of dollars for extras like new scrubs and continuing education (CE) courses, only to hear that team members didn't like the brand of scrubs or that they had to stay a couple of extra hours for training (even though breakfast and lunch were paid for that day). So, one day, I shared with the team the details of what we were going through for them, and I let them know:

> I want you to put yourself in my shoes for just a minute. Imagine doing the best you can and providing for your team, spending thousands of dollars on bonuses that go above and beyond to share in generosity. However, that is met with grumbling and complaints because some feel it's not enough or wish it was done differently. As a reminder the generosity here is not normal in the workplace. What most business owners do is take all the extra profits home and don't return the investment to their employees. A simple "thank you" would go a long way because a sense of entitlement is toxic and will not be tolerated. If you feel there's something better out there, then you're welcome to leave.

I admit I choked up a little when I told them, and when I looked around the room, real tears were being shed. But it was a turning point for us. Sharing my heart in that instance was really a good reset and a reminder that, hey, I'm a person too, and my feelings can be hurt as well.

Too much of anything is a bad thing: too much sugar is bad for the teeth, too much leeway may be bad when raising a child, and untethered generosity can create a toxic culture. If you get to the point that you've created a culture of entitlement, where generosity and bonuses are expected and never enough, then show your heart to make sure that your team knows that your generosity is all about them, but you're a person with feelings too.

Let's face it: it can be tempting to take advantage of the situation when someone is being generous, so as the leader, you've got to remember that it's a business and it's ultimately got to run like a business.

The Parents' Corner

Whatever It Takes

Sometimes during treatment, the unexpected arises, at which point we're often asked by parents, "How much is this going to cost?" In many practices, the unexpected does mean additional cost for treatment, which is a good business decision. But at Sturgill Orthodontics, we try to determine the complexity of the case up front and explain that the fee is comprehensive. Then, if something arises, we have the clinical freedom to do whatever we need to do to make sure that the patients get the best care without having to be concerned about whether something is paid for or having to try to figure out treatment without increasing the fee. We just do it.

Whether it's an impacted tooth, or your child fails to wear their rubber bands, or they break an appliance, you're not going to have to pay an extra charge. That's what we mean when we say we're going to do whatever it takes to get you to the end result.

Practice Makes Perfect

- Before you try to build your culture, you need to self-reflect and figure out your own values. One of the worst things you can do is to try to build a culture that's not authentic to who you are.

- Before you try to show your heart, you need to know your heart. What matters to you? People receive love in different ways. For me, one way is through words of affirmation, someone expressing thankfulness or someone recognizing a good job on a hard case.

- When you know what matters to you, share that with your team.

- It's important to know how your team receives appreciation and affirmation. For one team member, that might be a cash bonus; for another, it might be a handwritten note; for another, it might be a day off to spend with their family. Instead of treating everyone the same, we try to individualize how we show appreciation and show that in the way they will receive it best.

- There are different groups you can join, whether formal or informal, that can give you some perspective and ideas for identifying your core values and then helping to build your culture. We belong to C12, which is a group of twelve business owners that meet once a month and give honest feedback to each other.

- Join "friend" groups of other business owners who are not dentists but share the same ethics as you.

- If you're really struggling to understand your values, ask your spouse or a good friend.
- A really good resource is one developed by Stanford professor Kelly McGonigal, PhD. With it, you choose five traits that matter to you the most, and then you share those with your team. You can also ask the team to choose five, and share them. By having a better understanding of what matters to each individual, you can begin to better serve them.

CHAPTER FOUR

People Want to Be Coached

AS THE LEADER OF A PRACTICE, it's part of your job to constructively coach other members of your organization to be better at what they're doing because it's better for the team, for your patients, and for the practice as a whole.

To get that going from the start, we pair new hires with a team member who will provide them with critical feedback as part of their orientation. We tell those new hires during orientation that the critical feedback should not be taken personally; instead, it's coaching by a tenured team member based on the way I want things done. It's different and a little challenging for some, at least at first. But I always explain that we do it that way because we want the new person to perform really well and succeed at this job. It doesn't mean they are failing; it's because we hold ourselves to a very high standard with no room for error.

As part of our culture, I also maintain an open-door policy to allow people to let me know when someone is not following our protocol. However, it took me a while to train myself that it should not always be up to me to take care of everything when someone reports an error in protocol. So, I also coach my team on how to approach someone about an issue. What so many people don't realize is that, when you're irritated about something or you see errors happening, and you don't bring it up right then, you're the one who's going to carry that burden. You're the one who will keep being bothered by what you saw and what you didn't do to resolve it. Now instead of immediately saying, "I'll take care of it," and finding myself in the role of "bad cop," so to speak, when someone comes to me with a problem, I can start by asking the team member reporting the issue whether they've talked to the person themselves.

Still, when team members know they can tell you about something and you will handle it in an appropriate manner, it builds trust between you and them. So, I find ways to bring up a situation in a way that the source is not revealed. For example, one time a new employee came to me to report that another new employee was not following the rules of sterility by putting on clean gloves and barriers in the proper manner. She felt uncomfortable mentioning it to the other new employee because she, herself, was so new. So I shared with her a keyword to say to me the next time she saw it happening, which would trigger me to walk around the clinic and witness it firsthand and then correct the situation by coaching the employee in the correct procedure. Sometimes it takes a little creativity to come up with ways to make sure employees feel safe telling you things without ruining their work relationships, but it's important for maintaining a culture where people want to be coached.

To avoid building a culture of cattiness, when I do end up talking with someone about an issue that was brought to me, I never start a coaching session with, "A person who works with you told me ..." I try to remember how I would feel if someone went to the boss to tell them about something I did instead of just coming to me themselves; I'm sure I would be mad at the person and lose trust in them. Work environments can be ruined, and wounds that can be hard to heal may be inflicted. Those two employees may never trust each other again, and they might even become vindictive toward each other. Instead of risking to create a toxic culture, I always make a point to create a discussion where I saw what happened firsthand to avoid throwing another team member "under the bus."

Hire People Who Want to Learn and Grow

When you're working on a patient, the assistant who's standing right beside you is truly an extension of you. If they can anticipate your next need and deliver it to you without you having to ask, it creates an effortless flow. They anticipate your needs because they know how you work, they see what you're doing, and that frees you up to keep focusing solely on what you're doing for that patient.

In our office, that means coaching assistants on every detail, even something as small as passing instruments to me pointed a certain way. That may seem like a small detail, but I realized pretty quickly that my team wanted to know how they could improve because they wanted to make sure that they were doing their job well. When everyone is doing their job, it makes working alongside each other more enjoyable for both the assistant and the orthodontist. (Of course, doing a better job also makes it more likely that they will get a raise and their job will be more secure.)

If you hire people who want to grow and learn how they can do their job to the best of their abilities, then they take feedback in a positive light. "Thanks for letting me know. I want to know more. Tell me more." They want to learn to do their jobs to the best of their abilities. They want to learn new tasks, new techniques. No one wants to be stagnant in their role. But if you hire people who just want to do the minimum possible during the day, their response to feedback will never be taken in a positive light. "Ugh, one more thing I have to learn. It's never enough." That kind of person is not good for your culture, so you need to let that person go or, as we call it, "promote that person to a different practice."

As the leader of the office, aren't you always improving? Don't you read books, go to lectures, and spend time thinking about how to improve the practice? Then why wouldn't your team want to do the same? And they're looking to you to tell them how. While we're a practice that provides training and we work with individuals to help them learn how everything works, we are also sometimes able to work around lacking abilities for those team members who really try, have the right heart, and are a good fit for our culture. Conversely, we've seen people with the right clinical ability just never seem to fit in with the culture; someone may have great clinical skills, but if they're toxic to the culture, then they are not a good fit for our practice.

The Guardrails

Everyone performs well and feels more secure when there are guardrails—when they know they can't do something because it's not within the office standards. Within the guardrails, they're free to do what they need to do, and, as a team, we are able to move in the same direction. But when one person is going a hundred miles an hour straight ahead and someone else takes an abrupt left turn, then we won't arrive at the destination as a team. That's when you end up with people who are upset or lost, and it's all because leadership didn't clearly define the guardrails—where we're going and how we are going to get there.

Orthodontists often think that the problems with team members will self-correct, but that's not going to happen. That's wishful thinking or a desire to avoid confrontation. If you go home every night just hoping that your issue, whatever it is, will just spontaneously correct itself overnight, think again. Most issues never self-correct; they almost always need the leader to serve as the impetus for that correction. Otherwise, the problem is more likely to continue getting worse.

While, of course, the standard of the team is to act like adult professionals, every team is composed of diverse personalities and backgrounds. Each person perceives the world around them differently, so when communicating, what one team member hears may be a completely different point than what another team member hears. One of the key roles as a leader is to help identify when communication might have gone awry. Routinely, that can be communication between two team members, and your job, as the leader, is to coach on how that communication could have gone better. For instance, "Put yourself in their shoes. This is how it felt to them. I know you were asking that question just because you are curious, but because of their background, it was perceived as an insult that you didn't think they had done their job." In other words, I try to reframe it so that the people involved don't immediately think the worst-case scenario and instead are given the benefit of the doubt.

As your team grows and communication becomes more digitized, there will be an unfortunate loss of the tone and nonverbal cues that our brains so desperately need to truly understand the message from the sender. Because we're not receiving this message face-to-face, our brain paints the story of the tone behind the message. It fills in the details, sometimes perceiving words that are meant in a funny or caring way as insulting or degrading instead. "They're calling me out" or "They think I'm dumb," instead of, "They think it's funny too."

So we have to continually make sure everyone is aware of the difficulties with nonverbal communication and give those words the benefit of the doubt, and when in doubt, go talk to the person.

Getting and Giving Feedback

If you're married or have been in a long-term relationship of any kind, then you know what I mean when I say we all have had that experience of sensing that something's wrong with someone we love. You rack your brain trying to figure out what it could be; then, by the time they tell you, it's about something that you've been doing for the past year or five years or even longer. Something has really irritated them or bothered them all that time, and your first thought is, *Why in the world have you never said anything before now?*

We've all been on the other side of wanting to have feedback, and most of us have also had jobs where we weren't the boss and wanted to know where we stood. With no feedback, you're left to wonder whether you're about to get a promotion or you're about to get fired. That's because the lack of communication creates a sense of uneasiness and anxiety about the job. So, while it can be really awkward to give negative feedback, no feedback can be even more harmful.

That's why I coach all of my employees, and I've never had a coaching interaction where I gave feedback and later regretted it. I've also never had a coaching session where a team member said, "I wish you hadn't told me." The feedback has always been well received. Usually, the comments are more along the lines of, "Thanks for letting me know how we can work together to improve upon it." Earlier I talked about letting problems go on for weeks, months, or years and then suddenly giving feedback. There's no way to do that without it coming across as being very passive-aggressive, because it doesn't make sense that you wouldn't have said something sooner, so now it seems like you're only saying something to try to be mean. Compare that to giving someone feedback the day it's needed; I try to do it within the hour, and then it doesn't have that tone of passive-aggressiveness, and there's more a sense of being coached. "Here's where we missed the mark, here's how we need to make it better."

Clear and Direct Coaching

When it comes to coaching the team, you as the leader must be very clear and direct. Sometimes, members of the team will perceive conciseness or directness or attempts to clarify as rudeness or being militant. But if you explain expectations in clear language, then the team sees them as serious too, not just as something that is mentioned casually or something that you *hope* will happen. If you say that your expectation is something you want to see done, they often won't follow through; all they hear is a doctor saying, "blah, blah, blah." *Oh yeah, he mentioned that.* But if you say, "This is how we do it," and then follow through periodically to see whether the procedure or protocol continues to operate the way you explained, then you'll be able to see when it falls apart and be able to find out whom to hold accountable.

When you set clear expectations and explain why they are important, and it's your job to actually ensure they're implemented and then follow through, then the team will realize it's part of the culture.

In the clinic area of the practice, for example, when bonding a bracket to a tooth, it's all about what's called "isolation." That means if the tooth gets even the slightest amount of moisture, it can contaminate the preparation so that the bracket won't bond correctly. Even someone breathing in and out can create enough humidity to cause contamination. The reason that's so important is, if the bracket stays on immediately, that's only part of the success. The real success is for it to stay on long term. For a parent, it's obviously a huge inconvenience for them to have to take off work or to pull their kid out of school to come in to get something repaired. And those appointments are not profitable for the practice. We're seeing a patient to fix something, and nothing is being gained. Plus, patients are losing treatment time. So, it's frustrating and just a huge loss for everyone. The caveat here, of course, is when a patient breaks off a bracket because they are not careful of what they eat—some kids seem surprised that a bracket breaks when they have a consistent diet of raw carrots, ice chips, and fingernails!

One standard for us when bonding, say, a posterior bracket, or one in the back of the mouth where isolation is a big problem, is that team members know that I expect 100 percent isolation. That means we're putting in cheek retractors, lingual cotton rolls, and dry angle cotton, above and beyond what many practices may do. Even if the patient is 100 percent ready and it's not all in place when I sit down at the chair, I'll stand back up and say, "Come get me when you have that ready." Then the assistant knows it's not up to protocol and needs more preparation.

While it's really tempting for me to go ahead and bond the bracket, because it takes me about two seconds to make correction to what we call accurate, for me to do so would show the chairside assistant that we want it done a certain way but we'll let this slide. But if you walk away and they have to do the procedure over, and then wait on you to come back, then it's being done correctly, and that assistant will never again prep below protocol because it took so much longer and was a waste of time. Plus, they'll know you're really serious—this is the only way you're going to do a bond.

In the front of the office, there are also strict protocols, and team members are held accountable for following them. For example, we have a phone script for when a new patient calls. Occasionally, and randomly, I'll walk up to the desk and listen in to ensure they're asking all the questions and saying things that we want to be said. The script does not have to be memorized or necessarily have to be followed verbatim, but it's a checklist because no one is perfect, and, with so many other responsibilities in a day, no one is going to remember absolutely everything that needs to be said. As soon as the team member identifies that they're talking to a new patient, then they are to pull out the phone script and follow it so that they don't miss something. Just like bonding the bracket right the first time is more efficient, less frustrating, and less costly for everyone, the script helps ensure a more efficient, less frustrating, and less costly experience for new patients.

Having set standards is also very helpful when you have to change a protocol. If your team already knows that you expect something to be done and you're going to follow up, then they begin to hold themselves accountable.

That goes back to hiring the right people—the kind of people who will do what has been spelled out and explained as part of their job description.It may sound a little harsh, but a team that holds itself to really high standards will report problems when they see that someone isn't doing what's necessary or is not putting forth the effort, helping to identify when we need to help that person get a different job. That's different from when someone is truly trying and just needs more coaching.

Handling "Oops!" Chairside

It's really unfortunate, but so many times we hear about how doctors will call out a team member chairside, in front of the patient. An example might be a dental assistant saying "oops" chairside because of how that "oops" might be perceived by the patient. Usually the "oops" is something silly, like the assistant handed me the wrong instrument or dropped something—no big deal, and it doesn't impact the procedure. However, the patient might think "oops" means something went wrong in their mouth. Regardless of what the "oops" was for, or for any other mistake an assistant makes chairside, don't abruptly correct them in front of the patient. That just ruins that assistant's day and makes that parent or patient never want to work with them again because it makes them look incompetent. If someone is so incompetent that they have to be called out chairside, why are they working at your practice?

When you are working chairside, you are "on stage" in front of that patient or parent. They have nothing to do but listen to you and observe your every action, so professionalism should never be broken chairside. Of course, we're never going to allow anything to harm or hurt a patient, but in worst-case scenario, if I see that someone is not following protocol, I don't want to have that whole conversation with the assistant right there in front of the patient. Instead, I'll have that assistant switch out very quickly with another assistant, which they know means there's something really big that we need to discuss but not right now—we don't need to alarm the patient. Then later, I'll explain the situation to them.

We also use an acronym that I learned from a friend, Dr. Cole Johnson—LTA, which means, let's talk after. For instance, sometimes an assistant might ask, "Why are we doing this?" purely out of curiosity and wanting to better understand a procedure. But we might not want to explain right then because it would embarrass the patient. Other times, it might not be professional to explain something to the assistant in front of the patient, so I'll use LTA to have the assistant meet me in private to explain to them what they need to know.

The Value of Patient/Parent Coaching

Just as your job is to speak clearly and concisely to your team, it's also your job to speak in the same manner with parents and patients. Patients value being informed, and doing so can help alleviate stress on parents who might be second-guessing themselves about their role in treatment or whether they chose the right orthodontist. For instance, if home care instructions were not followed and now the treatment plan needs to be altered, assure the patient and parent that they will still have a great outcome, but moving forward will take a slightly different path.

Too often, providers don't spend enough time explaining why a child needs a certain treatment or the specific concerns that treatment is addressing. At the same time, it's important to be concise when explaining a treatment plan; taking too long to explain all the details of a plan can just confuse the patient and the parent.

On the flip side, if the treatment plan is really complicated, or yours is the fourth opinion that the parent has sought out, then it may take more time for them to understand what their child needs.

Otherwise, keep it concise so that the parent can go home and explain the needed treatment to their spouse and other members of the family so that everyone is on board. Often, that's where things get lost or confused, or a second opinion is sought, because the first provider didn't do a good enough job explaining to the parent, and then that parent was unable to explain to anyone else.

I also try to explain to the parent how their child's treatment compares to the norm to help them understand the "whys." That way, when they're explaining to someone else or comparing to another child's treatment, they understand why their child's treatment is different or costs more—or less. Parents talk to one another, and if they don't understand up front why their child's treatment differs from that of their peers, then they're left second-guessing and wondering whether they went to the right provider.

If a case is especially unique, then I'll spend a few extra minutes showing the parent x-rays and explaining why theirs is unique compared to a typical child's treatment. I'll even tell them if they look online, here's what they'll find, and while what they find may be true, here's why it's not true for their child. When you create that connection with a parent, and also physically have the records to show them why their child's case is different, then you can help them feel more confident in their decision.

The Parents' Corner

True Informed Consent

If you don't have a clear understanding of treatment, you should never be afraid to continue to ask questions. If you still don't understand what the provider has explained, then don't be afraid to get a second opinion.

As providers, it's up to us to use language and analogies that clearly explain treatment planning to you and answer all your questions. While we may understand the problem as "the maxillary arch is over constricted and that's causing reduced mandibular growth," you need to be told: "The upper jaw is shaped like a V and the lower jaw fits within that, and it can't move forward. It's like trying to fit your foot into a shoe that's too narrow—you can only go so far. But if we broaden the upper arch, we can bring the lower jaw forward. Just like if we broaden the shoe, your foot can fit into it better."

There is a multipage informed consent form that must ultimately be signed before we begin treatment. To me, true informed consent means the patient or parent really understands what they're agreeing to. When parents ask me questions, it makes me be a better coach and helps me learn to explain things better.

Practice Makes Perfect

- Everyone functions better when there are clear expectations and guardrails. They know what to do and aren't left wondering how they're supposed to do something.

- When it comes to coaching, sooner is always better than later. It's easier to set things right if you don't wait until the situation becomes awkward. Just rip it off like a Band-Aid, and then everyone can start to heal instead of letting something fester and then trying to fix it later. Waiting just leads to frustration and embarrassment, and then instructions don't seem genuine.

- Patients and parents also appreciate clear expectations. It may be awkward to explain that something is not going as planned with the treatment, but it's better to explain the negative impact that it's having on the child rather than wait a year and then try to explain why treatment didn't turn out as planned. At that point, everyone will be upset and understandably so, because it looks like you're hiding something. Just explain it when it happens, and then fix the problem.

- Whether you're talking to a patient, a parent, or a coworker, never underestimate the importance of speaking in clear and concise terms because vagueness can cause confusion and leave too many unknowns. Failure to do so with a patient or a parent may lead them to seek a second opinion. Failure to do so with a member of your team can leave them guessing about the standards and protocols of the practice. Then it's harder to make corrections with the team later because you were not clear about expectations in the first place.

CHAPTER FIVE

The Value of Autonomy

WHILE WE PROVIDE PLENTY of coaching and have protocols that we expect to be met, we also provide individualized autonomy on how those are executed.

Too many practice leaders—too many companies altogether—just don't give their employees autonomy, even when it would make for a more effective and efficient way to operate. They don't hand out autonomy because it relinquishes some of their control. Maybe it's a sense of pride or bravado from being the one in control; maybe they want people to come ask permission or ask questions constantly—that's how they get their sense of control.

One of the things that I grasped very early when I began to practice was watching the extreme inefficiency that comes from a lack of autonomy. I also saw a direct correlation between autonomy and job satisfaction. As owners of our own practices, we enjoy having autonomy; that's one of the defining terms of the profession—that you have autonomy to practice singularly. All of us thoroughly enjoy that perk and that benefit, and we forget to pass it along to those we work with.

Most of us have had some kind of job at some point where we weren't 100 percent in control, and we wanted to do more on our own because we all get joy out of making our own decisions. Our brains are made to make decisions. So, when we try to turn that off in our brains, then we just feel like a cog in a wheel.

Of course, there's also a risk factor in handing off autonomy. Is the person given the autonomy going to do the job correctly? It all goes back to hiring. When hiring, it's crucial to find someone who possesses the required skills and intellect to be trained in a manner that enables you to rely on them to function independently.

Everyone Makes Mistakes

Even with all the training in the world, people are going to make mistakes. It's really not a question of "if"; it's a matter of "when." That's the trade-off of efficiency.

Handing out autonomy is going to increase efficiency and job satisfaction, but the downside is that, along the way, there inevitably will be some sort of hiccup. That's going to happen because the decision that was made is different from the one you would have made. But if you have the right culture, you just learn from it and keep moving. I never want a hiccup to be something that is so criticized that your employee becomes fearful of making another decision. Instead, it's about teaching the framework in which they make decisions as they go through their decision tree.

As the leader, it's also about your ability to be fully open so that your team knows they can come to you when in doubt about how to handle a situation. In our office, some of the ways that we continuously implement autonomy is that we always tell people if they need to do something to make someone's day, they don't need to ask. If, for instance, a mom has had a really hard day and she is running late and the family's dinner is going to be late, a team member might give her a gift card to a local fast-food restaurant. They don't have to come in and ask. Or maybe a patient comes in, and they've lost their retainer, and they're going through a rough patch; the team is empowered to just give the patient a new retainer. I trust my team to make those decisions, and I will reinforce their decisions.

That's also part of autonomy—knowing that they are going to be backed up by me and by their leadership team, because the scary part about autonomy is that they're going to be stepping out on a limb. So, while they're out on that limb, they need to know that someone is going to be there for them if the limb breaks.

Having their backs, to me, also means doing things in a way that doesn't undermine them. For instance, if they tell me they made a decision about a patient and explain their decision tree, but then I disagree with their decision and want to do something different, I'll call up the patient to explain the situation but, again, in a way that does not undermine the team member. For instance, if they scheduled a patient further out than we want them to be seen, I'll just explain that the team member was unaware of something and that we're moving their appointment up; we're actually going to get them in sooner. Instead of telling the patient that the doctor disagreed with the team member's decision, we want to frame it in a way that doesn't imply that the team member is incompetent.

We also want our associate doctors to have autonomy and job satisfaction and feel like they're able to execute their profession and their goals of being their own practitioner, within our practice. Without that, they might always be second-guessing their decisions and worry that it's not the decision that I would have made. They might go back and forth instead of doing what they thought was right the first time; if they were to ask me, I might tell them to do the first decision that they made anyway.

With autonomy comes confidence to make decisions and know that those are the right decisions. If they're the kind of person who is always second-guessing every action they take, then either you have hired the wrong type of person or they just don't feel comfortable being truly autonomous.

I feel like the entire team should be an extension of me, and I trust them in the decision-making process. Sometimes a team member, or even another doctor, will start a conversation with, "I don't know if you're going to agree with what I did, but here it is." Even before I hear the story, I'll quickly let them know, "I'm sure what you did was great." I want them to feel comfortable in telling me the story. Even if I don't agree with their decision, I want them to know it is not going to be a hostile conversation.

Again, your team needs to feel comfortable being autonomous so that they have job satisfaction and the personal joy that comes from being your own person and being able to make your own decisions.

We've All Been There

We've all been through the kind of situation where you call customer service and the person on the phone just doesn't have the authority to actually solve your problem. Maybe you need to cancel a service, and they transfer you to the retention department, where you have to go through an attempt to save your account instead of just letting you cancel. Even though the first person you reached probably could have canceled your account with just one button in front of them, they're not allowed to do it. They have to transfer you to someone else.

Just imagine someone calling your practice and trying to make an appointment but being told, "Well, our scheduling coordinator is not here right now; they will have to call you." In one of the Ritz Carlton Customer Service training programs that I attended, I learned about first-contact resolution, where the entire goal is that the first person to interact with the customer resolves the issue. That made a lot of sense to me because I'm sure we've all had it happen when dealing with a big corporation, a 1-800-ABYSS number, where you have to know the code language of, "May I speak to a manager? Please escalate the call." You know that the first person who picks up the phone has no power, and you can even sense in their voice how frustrated they are that they have no control. It's no wonder the turnover rate is outrageous in those places, but it's because that company has just given up. It's just given up on hiring good people and training them and empowering them to solve problems. They're really just using them like pawns to filter callers to the next level, where maybe those people are trusted to solve the problem.

I purposely won't patronize places that have difficult return policies because some of those policies are just inconsistent and not customer-friendly. For instance, one clerk might give you a refund on a gift card that you can then spend on something else at the store right away, while another clerk will argue with you and deny you a refund or will escalate the problem to a manager who will or won't give you the refund.

Well, every time a customer has to tell their story all over again, they get more and more frustrated. We've all experienced this, and by the time you have to tell your story a fourth or fifth time, you're ready to be upset no matter who gets on the phone. Compare that to the

Nordstrom story where an employee took back tires even though the company did not sell tires.[2] Nordstrom is known for great customer service and for standing behind its products. Compare that to a company where it's like pulling teeth (a term I really hate to use as a dentist) to deal with their customer service department.

The solution is training. With our team, we tell them they need to try to resolve patients' concerns as their first point of contact. If a person comes in and they're upset, then the team member needs to try to figure out what it is going to take to get that person's concern resolved. They need to try to deflate the situation, not escalate it to an office manager or doctor where the patient then has to rehash the whole story. Don't escalate the problem because then the customer's frustration is also escalated.

The same thing applies when the patient is in the chair. If I come to the room and the patient is agitated for whatever reason, the first thing I want to do is figure out how they can be deescalated. I'm not going to delay and say, "We'll deal with this later" or "Let's get you back another time." All that does is make the patient feel less heard. Trying to punt the problem just takes more time and wastes more time.

At our practice, we really talk about setting expectations. Sometimes, I think, letting patients know what to expect is perceived as being confrontational, but it's actually the opposite. For instance, most of the time they would prefer to know that their appointment is running late because their day is so fully scheduled that a delay at our office is going to completely disrupt their day. If that happens, they sometimes would rather know about the delay and just reschedule. They

---

2   "The Nordy Pod: The truth about Nordstrom's legendary tire story,"
      Nordstrom Now, news release, accessed August 14, 2022, https://
      investor.nordstrom.com/news-releases/news-release-details/
      nordy-pod-truth-about-nordstroms-legendary-tire-story.

may be a little perturbed, but they're usually thankful to be told up front rather than find out later and then be late for their next appointment.

The Parents' Corner

Setting Expectations

In addition to the training that I've taken, I've learned about customer service from personal experience. Whether on a phone call or in a restaurant, hotel, retail outlet, or other place, when I've had a frustrating experience as a customer, I want to make sure that people don't have that same experience in my office. When I have a good experience, I try to dissect it to determine why it was a good experience. How was I greeted? How was I served? How did the establishment make my service their responsibility?

Then I try to translate that to our office. How can we improve the customer experience? Few things make people more uncomfortable than the unknown. If someone walks in and we're really behind, we tell them so and let them know how long we expect the wait to be. Then we'll offer them a cup of coffee, let them know they can run a quick errand if needed, or even offer to watch their child if they need to go pick up another child. We've found that patients prefer that kind of information to just leaving them in the dark. It's irritating to sit there for thirty minutes when their expectation was to be immediately brought back to the clinic.

The Framework for Decision-Making

To help your team have a framework for decision-making, make sure your mission, vision, and core values are all set appropriately and that everyone understands how to apply them.

Our mission is "Serving Others. Creating Smiles." When reflecting on that, we have to ask ourselves: Did the interaction we just had with someone make their day? Or did it just worsen their day?

Our values statement is as follows:

- Safety: I ensure patients, parents, and coworkers are always safe.
- Courtesy: I go above and beyond expectations.
- Show: I ensure that I am personally "show ready" and so is my area.
- Efficiency: I use my time and resources wisely.

We put the values in order of importance. Safety is first, and that applies, for instance, if someone calls and they're in pain with a tooth or implant. That's part of their dental health safety, so we need to get them in and get them taken care of. Or there's just generalized safety; for instance, a spill on the floor that needs to be cleaned up right away so that someone doesn't fall. Courtesy is about going above and beyond expectations; we don't want to just do what's expected. For instance, when an appointment is being made, we might offer to print a school excuse or put the patient on a cancellation list so that they can potentially get an earlier appointment and be seen sooner. It's thinking about what would be really helpful for that patient. That might be a coffee to go or maybe an umbrella if it's raining.

Show is about being personally ready and having the work area show ready as well. I'm a bit of a fanatic about cleanliness and order in the entire office. Nothing makes me crawl on the inside more than checking in somewhere, like at a doctor's office, and seeing someone sitting there with a dirty or cluttered work area. I remember checking in at a hospital once, and the facility itself was beautifully designed, but the lady doing the check-in had a cubicle littered with random Post-it notes, stickers, flowers, and a giant cup of soda—just really made herself at home. But to me, the patient, it didn't make me feel like it was a well-organized office.

In our office, there are no Post-its at the front desk; if a label is needed, we have a label maker. Post-its are temporary; they are not made to permanently adhere to a wall or the edge of your computer. Instead, every desk has a little whiteboard where the team member can make notes while they're on the phone, and then they can erase the notes as the task is completed. No little sticky notes to be passed along or potentially lost in transit. Coffee or other drinks are to be kept under the desk, out of view of patients. Each workstation has one picture frame, all of them matching, where the team member can have one photo inside the frame. When a job is a little messy, such as sorting the mail, it needs to be done and put away. Workstations are to be kept clean and free of clutter because patients are looking down over the counter, and they can see the worktop. Again, patients have nothing else to do but observe, so we want them to see that they are putting their care in the hands of a clean, orderly office.

As I write this, we're having to change one of our cleaning procedures: we have a therapy dog, and the other day I saw a clump of fur in the waiting room where he likes to hang out. It means vacuuming more than twice a day, even while patients are in the waiting room. But that's OK; I would rather hear a quick vacuuming being done than see a ball of fur where patients are waiting. Imagine being a patient, looking around and seeing fur on the floor: Would you feel like you were in a clean office?

Even if our standard protocol is to vacuum twice a day, by setting expectations of always being show ready, and giving team members autonomy, they can make the decision to vacuum more often, even if it means making a little noise around patients.

Our final value, efficiency, goes back to issues like escalating problems. Not only is the patient or customer going to be more irritated every time they're having to go up the ladder, but that is also such a huge waste of resources. Instead of one person spending ten minutes to resolve the problem when it is presented to them, escalating means another person has to spend time trying to resolve the problem, then another person, and then another. Soon, the whole office is stressed out about one problem, and an hour of employee time has been spent on it. At that point, the patient is probably never going to be happy because they are so irritated by having to go through all the rigamarole compared to one person nipping the problem in the bud right off the bat.

Employees represent more than just a dollar cost; there's also a time value to consider. Let's say a team member quoted $200 for a retainer replacement during a phone call with a patient. But when the patient comes to the office, we realize it's actually a different situation than what the front desk understood over the phone. That replacement is actually $350, a pretty big difference. The front desk staff member is instructed to share with the patient that the fee is different from what they were quoted because of a misunderstanding; for instance, the team member understood that a clear retainer replacement was needed (at $200), but what really is needed is a Hawley retainer (at $350). Most patients will understand and be fine with paying for the retainer that they need. But some get a little upset: they might say they can't afford the $350 and can only afford the $200 that they were quoted. At that point, rather than get into an argument with the patient, we just tell them that we will honor the quote, but if another of the same type of retainer is needed in the future, then it will be the $350.

We do it that way because it costs more in bad relations to argue with the patient at the front desk where others might hear, or to call in another manager and take up their time, than it does just to meet the patient's expectations right then. Plus, by having an argument with the patient, we end up with someone out in the community sharing their frustration about their experience. Instead of a problem that costs us $150, we could now be losing tens of thousands of dollars. Just that patient alone may never bring another family member in, but then imagine how many other people they might influence. We're not in the business of making an income off of retainers; we're in the business of doing orthodontic treatment, so we're not going to shoot ourselves in the foot over a $150 mistake.

Too many practices lose a lot of potential growth because they focus so intently on the negative. They worry about losing a few dollars of income when they can instead benefit from free advertising by patients as a practice that stands by its word.

Employees also see it, and they know your practice as one that gives them the autonomy to make decisions but also stands behind them when they make mistakes. The value of your team seeing their workplace in this light is incalculable.

Practice Makes Perfect

- Coaching and protocols set expectations, but individualized autonomy also empowers team members to meet expectations.
- Autonomy increases efficiency and job satisfaction, but it also inevitably means mistakes will be made. When it happens, keep moving, and don't be so critical that the person who made the mistake becomes fearful of making another decision.
- Every time a customer has to repeat their story, they get more frustrated. Giving your team autonomy allows them to deal with problems from the first contact.
- To help your team have a framework for decision-making, make sure your mission, vision, and core values are all set appropriately and that you understand how to apply them.

CHAPTER SIX

What If It Was Your Child in the Chair?

WHILE MISSION AND VALUES guide decision-making in our office, one perspective that underlies all decisions is: "What if it were my child in the chair?" Every decision should be made from the point of view of taking care of someone very near and dear. Whether it's a supply, a piece of equipment, hiring a team member, aligning with another doctor, a procedure or protocol, or a complicated treatment plan, we always ask: "What would I do if this were my child?" By always looking at decisions through that lens, you can go to bed at night knowing that you're doing the best you can for your team and your patients.

All of us would like to think that our providers are always going to do the same thing they would for us or our child as they would if it were their spouse or child in the chair. However, we live in an imperfect world where we can't blindly trust that everyone acts in the best interests of others. Some providers make decisions based on what is easiest for them, or most profitable, or maybe on some other kind of incentive. Maybe they have a close tie with a product or service—one which creates loyalty to the product or service exclusively. In short, there's always the potential for ulterior motives, with the most common being ease or profit.

Making the Right Decision

One of the things that helps me make right decisions is something a treatment coordinator once said to me. The treatment coordinator is the person who reviews treatment with patients and goes over financing, scheduling, and consent with them, and one time she said to me, "It's just so easy to follow up with parents after you because you just have so much confidence. You can look them straight in the eye and tell them exactly what we're going to do, what the plan is, and how we're going to follow through. And it's all going to end in a great result."

Some of that confidence stems from the fact that I know that what we are doing is the best. As a provider, we don't do things because we are trying to be more profitable; being more profitable just happens to be one of the side effects of doing the right thing. When you have more confidence, you actually have more people who trust you.

But that confidence actually stems from doing the right thing throughout the practice. It comes from being able to trust my team, and that starts at the front desk. I trust that the interaction patients have with the team at the front desk is going to be the best interaction they can have, my clinical assistants have the best skills that a patient can interact with, and the doctors are going to create the best treatment plan that a patient can have.

Chairside, I know that the products that we're choosing to use for that patient are the very best available. We're not skimping on brackets or other products because they're cheaper. We use products that are three to ten times more than the ones other practices may use because they are the most comfortable, the most durable, the most sterile—simply the best for the patient.

We take the same approach with treatment planning. Sometimes we're looking at a really hard case and trying to decide between two options, one of which is a lot more challenging. That more challenging treatment is the better treatment, but it's also harder to explain to the parent. Instead of taking the easy route and just telling the parent, "Oh, this will be so simple," I'll think about my own daughter and ask, "What if this were my daughter and I needed it explained to me?" If I were the parent, I would want to know, so I will at least take the time to explain the more complex treatment. They may decide not to do the treatment because of the costs, but at least they're informed.

So, for instance, I may have to explain why we recommend an implant for a child's missing tooth instead of just moving teeth to close the space. I'll explain how the more complicated treatment plan will age better and provide better lip support, and I give all the reasons why I truly believe it's best, and then I tell them this is what I would do if it were my decision. But I also realize there are a lot of things that factor into a parent's decision to move forward with a treatment, so I'll offer an alternative plan as well. That way the parent at least knows the pros and cons. And what I have found is that more than nine times out of ten parents will go with the more complicated treatment—even if they know it's more expensive, will take longer, and is more complicated—because they understand the advantages I've laid out for them.

Sometimes, though, I get frustrated because the parent is coming to us for a second or third opinion after having gone somewhere else, and the other orthodontist has suggested something that I know is easier for them to do. Maybe they suggested the treatment because they thought it would be an easier sell, but they didn't project their confidence in the treatment (knowing that a more difficult treatment would be better) and the parent picked up on that.

That's why I always present treatment options from the perspective of what I would do if it were my child, and I'm honest about it. I think it goes back to that extra sense I mentioned in chapter 2 (see the Parents' Corner) that moms in particular seem to have that lets them know that something isn't quite right.

The Same Quality of Treatment— No Matter the Patient

If you're a provider trying to grow your practice and you need to increase profit or margin, the last place to look for savings is in the quality of materials and service. Now, saving money on trash bags should not negatively impact the practice. But skimping on products and services that impact the patient is not the way to grow.

I once knew a provider who used a cheap eBay bracket on all of his patients, but when his own children need braces, I'm sure he'll buy something better for them. Unless I'm doing something like testing out a product, I don't use something different for family members than I do for patients. I use the same premium products on everyone.

The Parents' Corner

Who Would You Send Your Child To?

There are some great dentists out there who do some fantastic work. And some of them also do specialty work, such as root canals or orthodontics. But before a parent allows a dentist to do orthodontics on their child, I think a great question to ask that dentist is, "Who did your kid's braces?" The majority of the time, if the dentist is honest, they'll tell you that they took their child to an orthodontist.

As a parent, if you're ever unsure of the procedure being recommended, if the provider doesn't seem super-confident in the treatment they're offering, then maybe consider consulting a specialist. Don't be afraid to ask any of them, "If your child or your spouse needed treatment, who would you go to?" And then watch their reaction—that will tell you all you should know.

That goes back to treating every patient like it's your child in the chair. My wife, for example, has been in braces several times because she's not good at wearing a retainer, and she knows that she can just keep coming to me. But when she comes in, she doesn't choose one specific chair, one particular appliance, one particular bracket system, one particular assistant. She can sit in any chair, and she'll be treated like any other patient; we're not pulling out any kind of special appliances or brackets, no special assistant. She's getting treated just like any other patient; she's getting the best treatment, which is what we do for every patient.

We also give the best treatment even when it's someone who has been identified as in need of discounted or free treatment. That may be someone who, as I mentioned in chapter 3, simply can't afford treatment. Or it may be a family that has been identified as in need of free treatment through the Smiles Change Lives program that we participate in. Through that program, we've helped dozens of children obtain the orthodontic treatment they need to have the confidence to smile. For Sturgill Orthodontics team members, it's not only about trying to do the right thing, but it's also an opportunity for them to feel like they're giving back to the community. They're contributing to the free treatment that we give every year, and that adds value and purpose to know that they're a part of that.

No Cutting Corners

Even when treatment protocols are not being followed at home, we don't focus on placing blame over doing what's best for the patient. If the child isn't wearing their rubber bands as they should, we're not going to charge extra just because treatment isn't going as it should. Or, as I mentioned in chapter 3, if a patient ends up needing an appliance that costs more or we have to alter the course of treatment in a way that costs more, we'll just take care of that because it's what the child needs to have the best outcome. That's one of the things the other doctors say they love about practicing here—they're able to just do what's best for the patient, and there's never a discussion of how that relates to profitability. You don't find that at large corporate practices that will cut corners or limit treatment in some way to ensure a profit. Parents sometimes get drawn into ads that tout cheaper treatment, but unfortunately, sometimes you get what you pay for. The truth is, the practices are probably both making a profit, but the corporate one is doing it by cutting corners.

Sure, there are times when we could cut corners, but I often ask myself, "*Would I want my provider to do that?*" If the answer is no or in any way questionable, then we don't do it. Even when we're providing free treatment, we still ask, "What if that were my child in the chair?" One time, a company donated brackets that were not up to the normal standards of the treatment we provide. Although it was really generous of that company to provide the free brackets, and even though we were providing this treatment for free, we still needed to do it as well as we would for someone who was paying. So we switched to the brackets that we normally use.

If you create the right culture, even your team members will always be looking for ways to step up from the standard, not trying to find ways to step down from it. I'm not saying that we're not infallible. For instance, one time an assistant discovered that another assistant was getting ready to use an instrument that had not run the full cycle inside the sterilizer. There is a very small indicator that lets you know the cycle has been completed and it had been overlooked. As soon as the problem was discovered, we stopped the clinic and checked every instrument in every drawer (thousands of instruments) to ensure that any that had come out of that incomplete cycle were returned to the sterilizer and cycled through again.

Without having a culture that always tries to rise above standards, the employee who discovered the problem could have just stayed silent and went on about her day, or she could have decided that the instruments were "probably" sterile enough and then waited until lunch to say something. But instead, she stepped up and did the right thing. For her, there was no second-guessing. She reported the issue right away, even though it meant pausing the clinic for a moment and revealing the other assistant's mistake.

In fact, she put a stop to the problem, and the team jumped in and was taking care of it before I even knew something wasn't right. As a leader, that's the kind of team you want because you're not going to catch everything.

Interestingly, the assistant who caught the error left a practice where she was previously working because they did not have the protocol we have for sterilizing instruments. Their protocol involved using a high-strength bacteriostatic solution for cleaning, but not running the instruments through a sterilizer. How embarrassing as a practice to know that your employee is leaving because they feel guilty about your practice standards!

True, there are times that the team gets annoyed with me for the high standards, but they know that we're always going to do what's right and make sure we're stepping into the hard situations to give patients the best possible experience. When they see that in the practice culture, day in and day out, then there's no question about what to do when something is not right. Then your culture becomes self-reinforcing; tenured team members will step up and help new hires align to the culture.

Practice Makes Perfect

- Every decision should be made from the point of view of taking care of someone very near and dear. Ask yourself: "What if it were my child in the chair?"
- Focusing on doing the right thing at all times can instill confidence and build trust.
- Skimping on products and services is not the best way to increase profit or margin or to grow a practice.
- Deliver the same quality of treatment to all patients, from family to those treated for free.
- If you create the right culture, team members will always look for ways to step up from the standard.

CHAPTER SEVEN

Create a Safe Environment

JUST A FEW WEEKS BEFORE I wrote this, we had to let someone go who had been here less than ninety days because she wasn't a good fit for the culture.

In spite of all the worrying about what we had to do, after she was gone, there was an immediate positive impact in the area where she had been working. You could just sense the difference; everyone in that area had been frustrated and irritated. Individually, they were coming to me and telling me different concerns.

No one enjoys letting someone go; it's super hard, especially because you are ruining someone's day and sending them on to find another job. You know it's going to be hurtful. But in this instance, the individual just had a lot going on and wasn't able to participate as a member of the team—a key part of our culture. We even second-guessed ourselves when we were considering whether to let her go. We thought about finding her another role in the office. But ultimately, we knew what we needed to do; we needed to defend our culture. So, we made the decision, let her go, and again, everyone was able to breathe.

Even if it left that area of the office short-staffed, the remaining team members were happier and didn't mind working harder to make up for the shortage. When you feel confident that someone on the team is distracting or taking away from the culture you've created, then once you let that person go, the team will work better even when it's short one person.

Protect Your Culture

It's important to defend the culture of your practice. And when I say defend it, I mean from everyone. At times it can even mean from yourself. When you're a sole owner of a practice, it's easy to associate the practice culture with yourself. And while you have the greatest influence on your culture, you can also become someone who is a toxic leader or who is actually negatively impacting your culture. So, when it comes to protecting your culture, you have to include yourself in that scenario.

First, you have to defend your culture by protecting your employees, your work environment. Not only must they have the best and safest facility, an enjoyable workspace, but they must also be surrounded by coworkers who are team players and contributors, not energy vampires.

Your team needs to know that you're never going to let them be mistreated or abused by anyone, including vendors, patients, or parents. We discontinued our relationship with a vendor who was very hateful and rude to one of our employees. When it comes to vendors, we'll get our products from someone else, even if it costs more to do so, as long as it protects our employees from feeling disrespected. The same goes for abusive patients or parents. One time, a patient's father who was blatantly disrespectful was told that his daughter's treatment would continue, but he was no longer allowed to come to the office.

When employees see us actively defending their work environment and defending them, not letting them be taken advantage of by someone who makes their day more difficult, they'll feel like they're being protected. And when your team feels protected, you'll earn their loyalty, and they'll do anything for you.

Protect the Team—from Yourself

Again, when it comes to protecting the team, that means protecting them from yourself. At one point we were undergoing an office expansion while each doctor was also expecting a baby—it was a true perfect storm of scheduling conflicts. So there was real juggling of schedules to ensure patients were covered on top of all the other business-as-usual activities.

During it all, I found myself putting a ton of pressure on some of the members of my team, the ones who have been with me the longest and, therefore, are some of the closest. Just like when you're married, the people you're closest to—even in a professional relationship—are sometimes the ones you're hardest on. I found myself expressing my frustrations when things weren't up to standard; I thought, *I'm doing my job, why aren't they?*

Attitudes like these create really toxic leadership situations. I think all good leaders have the potential to go there because what makes a great leader is holding other people to a higher standard, being someone who speaks frankly and boldly, and having a big bandwidth of abilities and tasks. But if you have all those traits, there is going to come a point where that also becomes unhealthy because you start comparing what you're able to do or accomplish to everyone around you. Why can't they be at your level because that's what feels normal to you? But you're ultimately setting them up for failure and yourself for disappointment because you're expecting them to not only read your mind but also execute perfectly. They're obviously a unique human with a different set of strengths and things that they are good at—things that you're not good at—and that's why they're on your team.

That kind of unchecked pressure just leads to constant frustration, disappointment, and irritation—for everyone. Some of my longest-tenured, most loyal, best employees became really frustrated with me when I was putting undue pressure on them. When I finally realized what was happening, I went through stages of understanding. At first, I was frustrated and irritated. I questioned why *they* were frustrated—how could they feel that way when *they* were the problem! It didn't make any sense. Then I began to process: Was there any truth to what they were saying? I needed to consider the facts: It wasn't one person, it was several of *them* who were frustrated with *me*. And again, it was people who had been with me for some time, not new hires.

Finally, I reached a point of reconciliation. I sat with each person individually and had a super-frank conversation where I apologized for hurting and offending them. Then I listed the assumptions on both sides: I listed assumptions that they made that weren't true and then shared the truth with them; then I listed assumptions that I made that weren't true and asked them to tell me what the truth was.

Those were some very heartfelt conversations that, I confess, led to tears because I had wronged loyal members of my team. But I wanted them to know that I know that I'm not perfect; I'm doing the best I can, I need them on my team, and I'm willing to do what's needed to fix the situation and reconcile.

Stay Connected

We're moving forward now. For one of them, that meant reassessing her role. Her job had changed and evolved so much over time that I had her take a Working Genius[3] assessment, which basically evaluates what tasks give you energy and you're good at, tasks that you feel indifferent about, and tasks that are really hard for you. We discovered that her role had morphed—through her wishes and my approval—into tasks that she really didn't enjoy and wasn't good at. We found that she was actually better at other tasks that I suck at, which is important. She was trying to help me do things that are my strengths, which is automatic disappointment, while the things she is good at, and I'm not, were being left by the wayside. So, we refocused her role to be more aligned with the tasks she's good at and are looking at ways to take away distractions.

Sometimes, as a practice grows, the roles of the original team members evolve to the point that some of them jump ship. One reason for that is because they miss the relationship they had with the leader when the practice was smaller. There was probably more one-on-one, and it was almost like a family connection. When you're the leader, as your team grows, you may find yourself spread thinner among all the new team members and lose some of that closeness you had with the original team. Admittedly, I don't have the same connection with newer team members as I have with those who have been with me since the beginning, because when there are more team members,

---

3   "The 6 types of working genius," https://www.workinggenius.com/.

there's less of me to go around. Yet there's also less expectation of that close connection with newer team members; they basically get the same level of input from everyone—all the doctors and the other team members. So, they don't expect a lot of one-on-one with me.

Today I know it's OK to put more energy and effort into some of the original relationships because they don't want to just come in, do their job, get a paycheck, and go home. There is a different level of expectation with them, and having felt like they lost touch with me as a person was a little hurtful to them. Just a two-minute chitchat on what is going on in life means a lot to them—and to me. I always thought that they just talked to me because they had to since I'm their boss; I didn't realize they actually cared.

As the leader, you are a huge part of the culture. That means you can also be the person who is negatively influencing it. So you need people whom you really trust who will be your guardrails—people who have been with you for a long time and to whom you listen when they speak up because you know that they are not just trying to stir up drama.

To keep our culture from ever getting to that point again, I'm working on meeting with team members once a month to talk about what's going on in their area of the practice and what we need to do differently. We're also talking about things I'm not noticing because one of the assumptions on the team's part was that I see everything. How could I not notice something going on right in front of me? That was causing frustration on their part. But while they might be focused on something obvious to them, I'm focusing on three other issues and thirty other people while trying to keep our ship going in the right direction.

Keeping clear lines of communication—in both directions—is one of the most important and easily overlooked ways to maintain your culture. Your culture is kind of its own entity, and it is constantly influenced by who you bring on the team and by your leadership. If something's wrong with your culture, you have to always make sure that you're not just looking at the team, but you're also looking in the mirror.

The Parents' Corner

Let Us Know

As a parent, don't always assume that the doctors and managers of the practice know when something isn't going right or isn't a fit with what you know to be the culture. I've had patients who know me well enough to text me when someone at the practice hung up on them. Had they not told me, I would have never known, and that could have gone on for months or longer. After I promoted that individual from employee to patient (let them go), a number of patients told us about their bad experiences.

If you've chosen a practice or business that you know always delivers excellent customer service and has a great culture, but you experience the opposite of that, then let the leaders know. So many times, people don't want to speak up or complain, but we want to know about your experience. Remember that you have a voice that's valued because you're actually experiencing the practice as the patient or client, and that's something that the doctor or leaders never get to do. Please tell us and give us an opportunity to correct the problem.

Practice Makes Perfect

- Make sure you have a clear understanding of what your culture is.
- Clearly outline offenses to your culture.
- Do the hard things to defend that culture—even from yourself.
- Have people around you who are guardrails for how you're leading and reflecting that culture.
- Continually evaluate the pulse of your culture as it reflects each employee but be quick to remember your influence on the culture as well.

A Final Note for Clinicians

INDUSTRY CONSULTANTS WOULD LOOK at our practice and say, "You're offering more, so you should charge more." Well, maybe we could, but I remember what it was like to have parents who were having to really think about whether they could afford to pay for braces and that it meant not being able to pay for something else. I always want to make sure we're not just saying, "How much can we charge?" but making sure that we're charging something that is fair to the person who's paying it yet also allows us to be fair to our employees, who are working hard for their families.

That's something the team sees and also models. So much of your communication with your team is nonverbal. They see your demeanor when treating patients who are very affluent versus those who are receiving free treatment; they see whether you treat those families the same, and that continues to build your culture. Your team also knows how you are behind the scenes; are you always doing what's right? Are you cutting corners or doing questionable things that don't align with the values you espouse to the team?

The thing that has inadvertently helped us to have fantastic growth has been our focus not just on growing but also on how we can do things better, allowing us to grow organically from that because patients just know we care. You can't fake it, and your staff can't fake it. No matter how polite you might be, everyone knows the difference between genuine and disingenuous. You, as the leader of your organization, have to model that first, model it well, and model it consistently.

It's not always easy. In fact, it can be really hard to do. There are super frustrating days and patients or parents who can be infuriating. But you have to remember that you have people working for you, and all those people are sets of eyes staring at your every move and your every decision. And that will determine their view of the standard culture in the practice: *We do it this way, we don't do it that way, and we absolutely don't do it that other way.* You, the practice owner and leader, are the only one who can lay down those standards, and it's of paramount importance that that isn't forgotten and ultimately it can't be delegated.

That's why really large organizations fail at culture. Most people can walk in and tell when a dental practice is corporate-owned versus one that is owned by the doctor(s) providing care. The corporate-owned feels like you just walked into a big box retail store, whereas the doctor-owned feels more like a family.

If you're a doctor who owns your own practice, then your competitive advantage is that you are uniquely positioned to be in control of your culture. Where large organizations fail is trying to have someone lead the culture who is miles or states away or is trying to do it for thousands of people. That just can't be done well. What happens is every single location ends up having a slightly different version of that culture, and some of them are pretty good, and some of them are pretty bad.

I've been asked why we don't have twenty locations since we're so successful in our current locations. We could have expanded several times over the years, but I vowed I would only expand slowly to ensure we maintain our culture. Since we have the systems, I have no doubt that we could do that and do it well. But the sacrifice would be a diluted version of the culture that we have now, if not done carefully. What is most important to me is to know that what we've created is really good, but it's also really hard to continuously curate, nurture, and maintain.

The culture of your practice will never be stronger than the effort that you personally put forth. Your team's energy and excitement for any given day are only going to be up to your level; it is rarely going to surpass you. I often hear providers say, "My practice isn't successful because of the town I'm in," "I can't find good staff," or "because of the patients I have." While all those things are real factors in the success of a practice, what I don't hear enough are practice leaders saying, "My practice isn't successful because I'm not leading it well." Ultimately, it is true more often than not that the reason why your practice isn't thriving is that your personal leadership isn't where it should be.

I talk to a lot of providers who are frustrated because they know their practice isn't what they want it to be, but they're just staring at the trees and can't see a clear direction through the forest. If you need help getting your practice to the level where you know it should be, reach out to me to talk about a customized plan for your practice, just like we create a customized treatment plan for every patient. If you feel discouraged, burned out, lost in the trees, if you know that your practice and your culture aren't where they need to be, reach out to me at Sturgill Consulting, https://sturgillconsulting.com, and we'll help you find a pathway forward.

PART TWO

Culture and the Patient Experience

NOW THAT I'VE SHARED WHAT THE CULTURE inside Sturgill Orthodontics is like, let's look at how it impacts the clinical side of the practice. In this part of the book, I'll answer some questions I commonly get from patients and parents of patients. I'll discuss the value of treatment from a different perspective and how orthodontists are not all the same. I've also included some "Clinical Corners" specifically for clinician readers. And at the end of each chapter, I've included a summary of takeaways from the chapter, titled "Practice Makes Perfect."

CHAPTER EIGHT

Orthodontic Treatment—When Is It Needed?

ONE OF THE MOST COMMON QUESTIONS I get during a new patient exam is, "Does my child need braces?" While this question seems simple to answer on the surface, it is more complex than a simple yes or no. Let me explain.

For starters, there are several instances in which patients need orthodontic treatment to correct an issue that impacts their overall health or daily comfort. Some of these are as follows:

- a severely misaligned bite that makes it difficult to chew (masticate)

- a tooth that is impacted or trapped in the bone; without orthodontic treatment, the tooth will never erupt or move into place
- severe crowding that prevents all the teeth from erupting or lining up
- protrusive or flared teeth that prevent the lips from closing
- a crossbite, which is where the bottom teeth fit on the outside of the upper
- a severe overbite that prevents the lips from closing
- an underbite, which is when the lower jaw is positioned farther forward than the upper jaw
- a constricted or narrow arch that impacts tongue position and sleep quality

When it comes to timing the treatment for these kinds of issues, there is a lot of misinformation. For instance, there is some misunderstanding about the biology of teeth: some people think it's useless to have braces done early because teeth move later in life. In other words, they think if they have them straightened as a teen, and since their teeth are still growing, they will have crooked teeth as an adult. But if they wait until they are in their mid-thirties, their teeth will stay straight for the rest of their life. That's not the way it works. Without retention, teeth can grow crooked again, no matter what age the patient is treated with braces. Later in the book, I'll talk more about retention following treatment.

When Is the Right Time for Braces?

This is another question I'm often asked. Timing of treatment can make a difference—a pretty significant one. For instance, when a child is prepubescent, a few years can make a difference in whether the treatment is simpler or more complex. At age eleven, for instance, treatment might involve just moving some teeth to make room for others, but at age seventeen, there might be a need for tooth extractions or surgery.

Parents often don't know the best time to come in to have their child seen, and some are even inaccurately informed about the best time to visit an orthodontist, sometimes even by their well-meaning dentists. It's often assumed that it's best to wait until all the baby teeth have fallen out and all the adult teeth are in. But more than just straightening teeth, orthodontic treatment can address issues that can become long-term problems. These include issues like very deep bites where the lower teeth are completely covered by upper teeth when biting down, causing the lower teeth to be continually worn by the upper teeth. Even in young children, for instance, when there is a deep bite, we've seen wear on the lower incisors of a millimeter or more. Those teeth have to be in that person's mouth for a lifetime, so, by the simple math, if they lose one millimeter of tooth height in five years and the tooth is only eight millimeters tall to begin with, you can see how that's a significant problem.

We have seen patients in their fifties, sixties, and seventies who have deep bites that have never been corrected, and, over the years, their lower teeth have slowly worn down from being in tight occlusion with the top teeth. Even though the lower teeth continue to erupt to compensate for the constant wear, they're always touching the top front teeth. Eventually, the lower teeth get to the point that they fracture or break off. Then the person goes to the dentist to have them rebuilt, and the dentist has to explain that it can't be done. There's no room to put in a normal sized tooth to replace the worn tooth because there isn't enough space. That's when the person comes to us to move the teeth back to where they're supposed to be to create room.

And although they're happy with their results, they're also frustrated because they don't understand how they went so long without orthodontic treatment and why no one ever told them earlier in life that there was a solution.

I often tell parents that I'm not trying to scare them or convince them to move forward with treatment for their child, but when we see a problem like a deep bite, I let them know that it can lead to problems down the road. It may happen when the child is thirty or when they're seventy; we don't know when. But we do know that treating problems like a deep bite earlier in life can set up teeth for the best chance of longevity and help prevent the need for crowns, root canals, or restorative work as an adult.

When it comes to correcting your child's bite, having the adult teeth present is only one part of the equation. What also matters is where the child is from a skeletal growth perspective. Skeletal growth and dental eruption (teeth coming in) don't always coincide, and they don't necessarily coincide with age. There's a huge range. For instance, if a sixteen-year-old boy is skeletally mature but still has twelve baby teeth, then waiting for the adult teeth to come in will cause us to miss out on his growth opportunity. On the flip side, if a nine-year-old has all of his adult teeth in, but he is nowhere near skeletal maturity, then we would recommend waiting to start treatment.

Then there are patients for whom skeletal maturity doesn't matter all that much because they have a very good skeletal profile, meaning they don't have a large overbite, underbite, or crossbite—the kinds of underlying skeletal causation that we look to correct with orthodontics. With these patients, there's a larger time window for treatment; they could have pretty much the same result whether they were treated at age ten or age twenty because their foundations are the same at any age. It's like building a house really square and plumb and then just deciding when to paint it. There are those patients who just have good genetics and good bone structure and who could really be treated at any time.

That's why it's hard to give a blanket statement of when treatment should begin because it really is case dependent. For instance, a child may go through a big growth spurt at age eleven and it might be vitally important to start treatment on them because they have a huge overbite. If we don't correct it during that prepubescent growth spurt, which is the only time that kind of correction can be made, then they are locked in that overbite forever unless something drastic is done, such as surgery.

Timing is important because we have to take advantage of the prepubescent growth spurt, which can be vastly different for every individual patient. Just look across a room of middle-schoolers; especially in the sixth- to ninth-grade range, it doesn't take a minute to notice that there are kids at various stages of growth. *This child looks like she just came over from the primary school, that one looks like he's heading to college, I can't tell if that one is twelve or nineteen, and shouldn't he be in with the fifth graders?*

Because of genetics, everyone hits their growth spurt at different ages, and that's really key to orthodontic treatment. Many parents are confused by this variability. A friend of their child may be going through orthodontics, but their own child "isn't ready yet," according to the orthodontist. Or maybe a child was the first in the class to get braces, so the parent wonders, "Why so early?" Well, if the orthodontist is doing things properly, there should be a big range of ages among children getting their braces because that prepubescent growth spurt is an extremely unique time point that we're trying to hit for every patient.

The American Association of Orthodontists (AAO) recommends that all children see an orthodontist by age seven. This age is suggested because it is early enough to screen children for problems such as congenitally missing teeth or crossbites that, if not corrected, can negatively affect future jaw growth. In addition, this is the time when children enter into the transitional dentition (mix of baby and adult teeth), and how this time is managed can have a significant impact on how all the adult teeth erupt. By seeing a child as early as age seven, the orthodontist can begin continuous supervision and let the parent know when it's time to start treatment.

For the vast majority of patients we see in this age range, we take preliminary records to help us track the growth of the teeth and jaws, and then we place them in our Growth and Development program where we see them every three to twelve months, depending on what we are monitoring. Entering into this type of program is typically complimentary and offered by most orthodontists. These progressive records (photos and x-rays) are also very helpful to the orthodontist to see if a problem is worsening or getting better over time. This makes the decision process easier and treatment plans more accurate versus having a single time point of records on which to make decisions. But parents are often afraid to bring the child in at age seven because they think that automatically means they'll be put in braces. The vast majority of the time, braces are not put on at age seven, but this early evaluation allows us to identify other problems that need to be addressed. For instance, at age seven, we might find an impacted canine tooth that would ultimately require surgery to bring in. However, if caught early enough, that surgery can be avoided by just removing the baby canine; the majority of time this will allow the adult canine to come in. But if the parent waits until the child is twelve, then a lot more work has to be done.

Even if your child is twelve years old, it's not too late to see an orthodontist. In fact, it happens all the time. A direct referral from a dentist is not necessary either; you can still make an appointment with an orthodontist. Call your local orthodontist, and they can let you know what timeline is best for your child.

Even if you're seventy-five years old and have never seen an orthodontist, it's not too late. We treated a woman who was eighty-four years old when she had her first orthodontic treatment done, and she was the life of the party every time she came in. She had paid for her children and her grandchildren to all have orthodontic treatment and finally decided at eighty-four that it was her turn. She was thrilled with her new smile, and her only regret was not doing it sooner. Many times, adults assume that teeth cannot be moved after a certain age or they are too fragile or have too much dental work. That is seldom true. Teeth can be moved at any age, and, as long as they are healthy, moving them with orthodontic treatment causes no harm. We can even move teeth that have crowns, root canals, bridges, fillings, and veneers; even with dental implants, it is possible to go through orthodontic treatment.

Why Do Some Kids Have Two Sets of Braces?

When it seems like a child has had two sets of braces, what they're undergoing is actually known as Phase I and Phase II treatments. Phase I treatment is typically done on children when they are around seven to eleven years old. If a child needs Phase I treatment, it's because there is an issue so significant that, if not corrected early, it is going to be an even bigger problem later. Phase II treatment is more common and can take place from adolescence through adulthood; this is the treatment that most people identify as straightening teeth, although there can be much more involved in making corrections in this phase.

Clinical Corner

Treating When It's Most Beneficial

Some orthodontists advocate treatment even before age seven, but I have yet to see anything that can't be corrected at age seven, so we prefer to wait until the child can understand what's going on a little better. We find that's a little bit easier emotionally for everyone.

We try to be a very literature-based practice. So, while we pay attention to up-and-coming changes, we don't necessarily jump on those as a practice. We prefer to wait for more peer-reviewed studies. If those determine that there is a benefit to something new in treatment, then we will consider adding it to the practice.

There is a good chance your child's teeth and bite will not fall into one of the categories of problems that I listed at the beginning of the chapter. If that's the case, then why would they still need braces? That's when it comes down to the esthetics of orthodontic treatment—in other words, how the teeth look when smiling and in relation to the face. The next chapter describes how orthodontics is about far more than just straightening teeth; it's about making sure each patient's smile is one that is best suited to them for the long term.

In my practice, Phase I treatment is not always recommended because we are conservative in our treatment approach, and if there will be no harm done by waiting, we will complete the treatment all in a single phase at the appropriate time. However, there are certain situations when Phase I treatment is recommended because it can have a significant impact on future dental eruption, jaw growth, and esthetics.

At the beginning of the chapter, I listed several reasons for orthodontic treatment. Of these, one most commonly seen as a reason for Phase I treatment is the posterior crossbite, or a crossbite in the back teeth. It's important to correct this early because nearly all patients who have this crossbite develop what is known as a centric relation to centric occlusion (CR/CO) slide. What that means is that, when biting down, the patient has to move their lower jaw to one side or the other for the teeth to meet up. This CR/CO slide causes the lower jaw and subsequently the chin to be positioned off-center. That can impact future growth of the condyles (jaw joint) and can lead to an asymmetry in the growth of the lower jaw (chin to the side).

Another reason for Phase I treatment is an arch that is not developing optimally. An arch that is constricted or too narrow, which can crowd the teeth and the tongue, can lead to sleep problems. There's a mistaken belief that the jaws will continue to grow to make room for all the teeth, and that will alleviate crowding. But the arch form of the jaw that houses the teeth doesn't actually grow in length; any growth as an adult happens near the jaw joint. The jaw will grow forward and down, but it does not increase in size to make more space for teeth to grow in. In other words, the space that you have for your teeth at age nine is the space you're going to have for your teeth at age ninety. During Phase I treatment, an appliance known as an expander can create a little more space in the upper jaw, but this treatment only works in young children while the bone is still developing.

Phase I treatment, when recommended, is typically a year in duration and has specific goals in mind. It is very common for this treatment to be only on the upper teeth, but it can also be done on both arches. In addition, this treatment is customized for each patient, so some children may have just the four adult teeth with braces in the front, while others will have a combination of adult and baby teeth with braces to create the ideal biomechanics.

Once the goals of Phase I treatment are reached, any appliances and braces are removed, and everything is held in place with retainers. Since Phase I treatment is typically done before all the adult teeth are in, nearly all patients who have Phase I treatment will need subsequent Phase II treatment to achieve the ideal bite and esthetics as the rest of the adult teeth erupt.

One advantage of doing the Phase I treatment is that the length and complexity of the full treatment is decreased and major problems or even potential harm to teeth and jaw growth are corrected early.

Practice Makes Perfect

- Orthodontic treatment can correct issues in the mouth ranging from misaligned teeth, bite-impacted teeth, or crowding to arch development that can negatively impact tongue position and sleep quality.
- The right time for braces is unique to each person.
- Some patients are candidates for Phase I and Phase II orthodontics, which first address development and functionality, and then address esthetics and function.

CHAPTER NINE

The Smile Arc

ESPECIALLY IN AMERICAN CULTURE, having an unattractive smile seems to have almost become insufferable on some level. People who have an attractive smile seem to be more accepted in almost any situation than someone whose teeth are crooked or misaligned, worn or broken, or just generally appear to be in ill health. Over time, as orthodontic treatments have become more widely available to the mass population, it's just become less acceptable for people to have severe orthodontic malocclusions or misaligned teeth.

In fact, a study by the American Association of Orthodontists[4] found that there are greater social benefits to having a good smile and that people with ideal smiles are viewed as being more intel-

---

4   Matheus Melo Pithon, Caroline Carvalho Nascimento, George Caíque Gouveia Barbosa, and Raildo da Silva Coqueiro, "Do dental esthetics have any influence on finding a job?" American Association of Orthodontists, July 2014, accessed November 27, 2022, https://www.ajodo.org/article/S0889-5406(14)00623-4/fulltext, https://doi.org/10.1016/j.ajodo.2014.07.001.

ligent and more likely to land a job. The objective of the study was to determine whether dental esthetics influenced a person's chances at finding a job. It involved using photos of ten people, two photos of each person. One of the photos showed the person's actual teeth and smile, which were imperfectly aligned, and the other photo showed digitally altered versions of the person with straight teeth and ideal smiles. The photos were shown to two groups of hiring personnel for commercial companies along with questionnaires about the likelihood of the individual being hired and their honesty, intelligence, and efficiency on the job. While the results of the study found that a person's smile was not a significant indicator of whether they were honest or efficient, the photos of ideal smiles—at least according to the hiring personnel in the study—indicated that a person was smarter and more likely to be hired for a job.

Women, in particular, seem to understand the impact straight teeth can have on a person's life. Moms, we've found, tend to push for orthodontic treatment more than dads do; as I mentioned in chapter 2, they seem to have that extra sense about things. Dads seem to more often have the mindset—especially toward their sons—that straight teeth didn't matter to their generation, so why should it matter now? *I didn't have braces, and I'm fine*, they sometimes think. But in today's selfie-obsessed culture, where youth are constantly seeing how they look to others, it's not uncommon for them to notice something that's even a little off in their smile.

Even my staff have noticed the change in the way people perceive themselves over time. It used to be that kids only saw their teeth in the mirror for the few minutes a day that they were brushing, but they didn't spend a lot of time staring at them, looking for what they perceive as flaws. But again, today's culture really seems to be pushing the importance of the ideal smile as it becomes ever more focused on image. I'm not saying that it's necessarily a good thing for image to be front and center, but straight teeth are definitely a part of that focus.

It's actually easier for kids to go through orthodontics these days because more of their peers are also wearing braces at the same time; that wasn't the case a few generations ago. Our adult patients who did not have braces when they were younger often tell us they wish they could have had braces as a youth and "just had it over with." That would have allowed them to have had straight teeth for those impactful early years when going through school and college and getting a job—those years when gaining self-confidence and self-esteem are so important.

Improved smile esthetics has been proven to substantially improve self-esteem, which then has an impact on attitudes and personality when orthodontic treatment is complete.[5] In fact, in our office, we've actually seen people evolve their entire image as their smile improves. They smile more, buy new clothes, get a new haircut, become more outgoing—it's really an amazing transformation to see.

Research has also shown the opposite to be true, especially in females; teeth out of position, or malocclusion, has actually been correlated with negative psychosocial impacts for girls ages twelve to seventeen.[6] At a time when youth are developing their self-image and self-worth, and body image and the awareness of dental appearance are increasing, norms set by friends and peers can have a significant impact on a teen.

5   Gordon L. Patzer, "Improving Self-esteem by Improving Physical Attractiveness," *Journal of Esthetic and Restorative Dentistry* 9, no. 1 (1997): 44–46, https://doi.org/10.1111/j.1708-8240.1997.tb00915.x.

6   Eugene Twigge, Rachel M. Roberts, Lisa Jamieson, Craig W. Dreyer, and Wayne J. Sampson, "The Psycho-Social Impact of Malocclusions and Treatment Expectations of Adolescent Orthodontic Patients," *European Journal of Orthodontics* 38, no. 6 (December 1, 2016): 593–601, https://doi.org/10.1093/ejo/cjv093.

But teens aren't the only ones who feel pressure from peers and others. Studies have also clearly shown that the overall quality of life vastly improved in adults from the positive psychological impacts associated with oral rehabilitation.[7]

The results of these studies come as no surprise. You've no doubt seen someone who was self-conscious of their smile and maybe even watched them physically hide their teeth by holding up their hand or smiling with closed lips. It's sad to imagine training your brain to interrupt a moment of laughter or joy by remembering to hide your teeth. During a smile, our body activates twelve muscles, occurring in pairs:

- zygomaticus major pulls the lips up and back (variation causes dimples);
- zygomaticus minor pulls the upper lip further up, outward, and back;
- orbicularis oculi cause the eye to squint or crinkle;
- levator labii superioris pulls the lip and nose at the corner;
- risorius pull the corners of the mouth to the side; and
- levator anguli oris helps raise the angle of the mouth.

When those twelve muscles are activated, a jolt of dopamine, endorphins, and serotonin (the feel-good hormones) are all released.[8] That release also relaxes your body and reduces your heart rate and blood pressure. What a wonderful design God gave us by creating a biochemi-

---

7   Vanessa de Couto Nascimento, Ana Cláudia de Castro Ferreira Conti, Mauricio Almeida Cardoso, Danilo Pinelli Valarelli, and Renata Rodrigues de Almeida Pedrin, "Impact of Orthodontic Treatment on Self-Esteem and Quality of Life of Adult Patients Requiring Oral Rehabilitation," *The Angle Orthodontist* 86, no. 5 (2016): 839–845, https://doi.org/10.2319/072215-496.1.

8   Sarah Stevenson, "There's magic in your smile: How smiling affects your brain," Psychology Today, June 25, 2012, https://www.psychologytoday.com/us/blog/cutting-edge-leadership/201206/there-s-magic-in-your-smile.

cal response when we smile! But that experience can be immediately overturned when someone feels stressed about smiling; instead, their body responds by releasing epinephrine and cortisol (stress hormones). Understanding this hormone roller coaster makes it no surprise that patients have shown an increase in self-esteem and overall quality of life when they feel confident smiling. That confidence carries over not only to job and career success but also in finding a significant other.

What Is the Smile Arc and Why Does It Matter?

As orthodontists, we're often asked, "How does orthodontic treatment impact your facial appearance?" I've been talking about the impact a great smile can have on a person's life, and one reason a smile is so pleasing to others is because of what is known as the smile arc.

You've likely seen freestanding models of perfect teeth at the dentist's office; you'll see them around our orthodontic offices. Well, the goal is to get the teeth to look that perfect—but in each patient's mouth as it best fits them. This is known as the "smile arc." Achieving the pleasing and youthful smile arc, one that gives the patient the most attractive smile for their face, is one demonstration of the orthodontist's artistry.

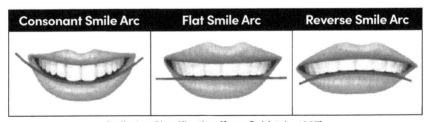

Smile Arc Classification (from Goldstein, 1997).

The smile arc is about intentionally positioning the front teeth within the lip opening so that they drape down and follow the line of the lip. We want to avoid over-flattening the smile, which is when the edges of the lips tip upward but the teeth are straight across. We also want to avoid a "reverse smile," which is when the canines look very long on each side of the smile while the lines along the bottom edge of the lateral and central incisors curve upward. The incisors are the four front teeth on top, and the canines are the longer teeth on either side of the incisors.

There's nothing wrong with the bite in a reverse smile—the person's bite will still function well, and their teeth are in a good place from a dental health perspective. But the artistic side of a smile has not been considered. So, while parents may choose treatment because it's cheaper or closer to home, all braces are not the same and all orthodontists are not the same. Ultimately, the teeth may be aligned, but there can definitely be a difference in outcomes—in the smile arc—from one orthodontist to the next.

Of course, not every outcome is the best reflection of an orthodontist's capabilities and artistry. If a child has braces but never wears their bands, never brushes their teeth, and ends up with cavities, the result isn't a fair reflection on the orthodontist.

While the term "smile arc" is not something people commonly discuss, patients and parents often say they don't want a smile that looks unnatural. They've seen some outcomes after braces that look like, well, fake teeth. They don't look real or natural. That's why I always encourage people to look at results when vetting orthodontists. If you're a parent asking your child's classmate or another adult, "Who did your braces?" then it's likely that beautiful, natural smile did not happen by accident. Smiles that make you go "Wow!" do not happen unintentionally. Or, if you ask around and it seems like everyone goes to the same office, including multiple family members, then that might be a good indicator of the orthodontist's outcomes. Basically, the results speak for themselves.

The Aging Smile

The smile arc is also about setting someone up to age well with their smile. As people get older, gravity has an impact on everything. The same thing happens to the lips; the upper lip lengthens, and the lower lip drops down a bit. When someone smiles, we love to be able to get them to the best point that we can within the limits of their biology and natural anatomy; sometimes there are limits to what we can do without doing something really drastic, such as surgery.

For instance, we like to see two or three millimeters of gum tissue during a smile as a teenager because we know that's going to turn into one and a half millimeters when the patient is in their thirties; then they will have almost no gum display when they are in their fifties, and they will still have a nice, youthful mouth in their sixties and seventies.

Compare that to someone who finishes treatment, and none of their gum tissue shows when they smile; you just see half of their top teeth. When that person is in their sixties, because of gravity and their lengthening upper lip, we're going to see hardly any of their teeth on top.

The angle of your upper front teeth also comes into play when determining the best smile arc. The teeth support the upper lip, so if they are orthodontically tipped down too much or retracted too far, then lip support is reduced. That can accelerate aging of the lips. In a borderline case, where extractions are being considered, we will err on the side of not extracting the teeth because they provide the support for the lips and make them appear a little fuller for a longer period of time. But we have to be careful of too much fullness because that can interfere with the patient's ability to close their lips, which, again, speaks to lip incompetence.

When it comes to extractions to accommodate all the teeth, we look at how that will affect a patient's appearance and function for the long term. If we go to the extreme and say "no extractions ever," then the patient may end up with too much fullness—in other words, teeth that are the first thing to enter the room. That's not only unattractive, but can also impact breathing and speech. Plus, when a person has to force their lips to close, they can end up with what's known as *mentalis strain*, which causes their chin to disappear. Patients who have this often think they need jaw surgery to bring their chin forward, but the problem is just that their chin disappears because they're straining their mouth so much to cover their teeth. Our practice removes teeth as part of treatment but only when it's absolutely indicated for the most attractive smile and most functional bite.

More Than Meets the Eye

Parents sometimes wonder why they only see the orthodontist chairside for a few minutes while their child is going through treatment, so these are all of the things we're processing in those few minutes: first, if the teeth fit well from a model perspective; next, if there is anything specific about this case that we can modify, such as tooth shape, gum margins, or height of the tooth; and then, we look at the smile from the front to see whether the midline matches up with the nose, the function of the jaw matches up with the face, the smile fits within the frame of the lips, how much gum is showing, and more.

When we orthodontists are chairside, we really home in on the teeth themselves to examine how everything is moving and fits together—sort of like those freestanding models of teeth that I mentioned. When we're sitting there chairside, pulling the patient's cheek back and asking them to bite down, we're looking very closely at the teeth themselves and the mechanics of how everything will work when treatment is complete. And that's important. But with all that close-up examination, one thing that can get missed is the esthetic component. How will the patient be perceived in a face-to-face conversation? Sitting beside the patient leaning back in the chair and looking into their mouth, their teeth may look awesome. It may look like treatment is done. But after sitting them up and then looking at them from the front, it's sometimes clear that work still needs to be done.

That's one thing that sets Sturgill Orthodontics apart. We take the extra time to examine patients from the front so that we can see what others see, so that we can see how the patient will interact when they see themselves in the mirror, when they meet people. Because that's what matters to them. They don't care how their teeth look when their cheek is pulled back and they are asked to bite down.

Dealing with the smile arc is also about getting the real smile. For instance, sometimes it can be tough to get a teen or a shy person to display a full smile, so we have to get them to show that to us. And some patients who have, say, a very gummy smile will train themselves to not show their full expression. So, I always try to get patients not only to laugh to connect with them but also to see what their smile really looks like. When someone is really cracking up from hearing a corny joke, we might then realize that they have an inch of gum showing. That's when we say, "Ah, the curtain went up."

We take pictures of patients for their charts, and everything might seem normal, but when we get them to relax and show us their true smile, that's when we know their treatment plan may be drastically different, and we want to catch that as early as we can.

The Best Fit

As with many things, there can be extremes in orthodontics. Some orthodontists say that no matter how well a person's teeth fit together, they're going to wear them down, or they're going to have jaw problems no matter what treatment is done. Another extreme is the orthodontist who says a tooth even a fraction out of place will create problems. Well, both of those are right. No matter how your teeth fit, chances are, over a lifetime, you're going to experience changes with the shapes of teeth and, consequently, their function and occlusion. Also, temporomandibular disorder or dysfunction (TMD) is so multifactorial, it cannot be solely attributed to bite changes. Orthodontic alignment can only help prevent a worse temporomandibular joint (TMJ) problem but cannot claim to prevent one from occurring. We just don't know which patients are most at risk.

Opposing teeth are supposed to interdigitate; they should lock together like a zipper. For example, the edge of a tooth in the upper jaw should fit nicely into a groove of a tooth in the lower jaw. Unfortunately, a lot of patients have teeth that naturally fit edge to edge, and that point of contact is where more damage from wear will occur. But I've seen patients in their sixties whose teeth are textbook tip to tip (an incorrect bite), yet they are not worn down. And then there are patients who had braces as a child, and their bite fits great, but they have still worn their teeth due to excessive grinding without wearing a nightguard. When looking at an eleven-year-old, it's hard to know which patient they'll grow up to be—one who never wears down their teeth no matter what or one who will wear down their teeth even though they fit together perfectly. Our goal with orthodontic treatment is to give every patient the best chance for success, and that means getting their teeth and jaws into the ideal position for the long term.

Clinical Corner

What Is Your View of Patients?

Do you look at each patient's teeth from the front before taking off their braces? It's a simple step to take but crucial for achieving the best smile arc. If the only view you've ever had of the patient is from above and upside down while they are in the chair, then you may be missing the bigger picture. To achieve the ideal smile arc, at Sturgill Orthodontics, one of the things all of our doctors do near the end of treatment is have the patient sit upright in the chair. We then come around to the front and look at them straight on. Then we have them talk to us so that we can watch how their teeth fit within their lips as they're speaking, smiling, and sitting face forward. We want to see them as they will see themselves in the mirror and as others will experience their smile.

Practice Makes Perfect

- Especially in American culture, having a perfect smile has become the new norm.
- Studies have shown that people with an attractive smile are viewed more favorably and even given more opportunities.
- The smile arc reflects the orthodontist's artistry.
- The smile arc is about intentionally positioning the front teeth within the lip opening so that they drape down and follow the line of the lip.
- The smile arc is also about masking the effects of aging on the face by creating a youthful smile.
- A final assessment of the patient from a face-to-face perspective is an important final step to determine if small adjustments at the end of treatment are needed to perfect the smile arc.
- Teeth are going to move and change with time, so the goal of orthodontics is to give teeth the best chance of looking good and functioning well for the long term.

CHAPTER TEN

Braces and Aligners

WHEN IT COMES TO THE MODALITIES used for treatment, there's an analogy that describes many practices pretty well: when you're a hammer, everything looks like a nail. Sometimes practitioners get so deeply involved in what they think is the most appropriate type of treatment that it's all they talk about in a consult. For instance, if you are vetting providers and the majority of what you hear from the orthodontist, treatment coordinator, or staff is about the product that the practice uses, then it might sound more like they're selling a product than a profession. At some point, providers who focus solely on one type of tool, in my opinion, go a little off the rail and it becomes more about how far they can push the boundaries of the tool and less about what is best for the patient.

In our practice, we try not to pigeonhole all of our patients into the same type of treatment; instead, we use a wide range of modalities to treat patients because we treat a wide variety of cases—various ages with various malalignments, malocclusions, and social and esthetic concerns. Our decision tree does not typically boil down to something as simple as braces or aligners; it's usually (1) what is best for that patient's overall health, (2) what is best for their face type, (3) what is best for their jaw, (4) what is best for their smile, (5) treatment time; (6) comfort, and (7) patient preferences, which gets down to little things such as whether the braces will be clear, silver, gold, etc.

Our culture is to decide modalities based on what's best for the patient and not about having bragging rights to a colleague about how a modality was used on a complex case or how can we increase our numbers on a certain product to get recognition from a large company. That means sometimes we have to tell patients what they don't want to hear. Sometimes they come in, and we're their second or third opinion, and they really just want something like clear aligners on top to fix one tooth. I thank them for sharing their concerns but then explain to them why they actually need something more— maybe braces or even jaw surgery. That's an extreme but real example. I explain how it's going to change their face and their airway and improve their overall dental health. They may only be concerned about one tooth, but they're going to spend a fair amount of money for a minor change when, for just a little more, we can fix so much more than a singular esthetic concern.

The job of the provider is to explain, in an easily comprehendible way, what's going to achieve the best result. What we've found is that patients rarely end up going with the simple solution they thought they wanted, even if another provider down the street offered it to them. I believe this goes back to our culture and that extra sense that people have. They know when we're being genuine and telling them what they need to hear—even if it's something they probably don't want to hear.

Creating Compromises

We customize the modality for every patient based on three things: (1) the treatment goal, (2) what modalities will allow us to reach that goal, and (3) patient choice. Notice that patient choice is last in the list because we do not want to introduce compromise into the treatment plan when really it is not an option. The problems come when the provider gets those three elements out of order and places patient choice first and then tries to create a treatment goal within that patient choice.

If a patient has a straightforward case, meaning they truly just need some kind of straightening, then that person will have an array of options to choose from. Those choices might include metal braces, clear braces, clear aligners, in-house aligners, and lingual (behind-the-teeth) braces. We'll talk to them about the pros and cons of each, such as required level of compliance, comfort, speed of treatment, esthetics, appointment intervals, and appointment length—feedback from that kind of information helps us understand what is most important to the patient.

If the case itself is more limiting—a correction in a child that needs to be done now, not later—then we don't offer options to avoid introducing compromise into the treatment plan. *This is the treatment that is needed; these are the modalities, and the treatment is needed now.* I think this is where some orthodontists run into an ethical issue.

For instance, a child may present with a crossbite, and the orthodontist lets the parent choose aligners as a modality when the best outcome would be accomplished with an expander and braces. In a case like this, we won't even offer aligners, even if the parent tells me another orthodontist said that was an option. I feel it is my ethical responsibility to provide only what's best and aim for the best result possible given the limited window of time in which a correction of that magnitude can be done. Otherwise, the correction later in life is more difficult to achieve and may be more costly and time-consuming.

Now, if the patient is an adult, then we can talk about a compromise. For instance, a sixty-year-old who knows that it is too late to fix their crossbite without surgery and wants to correct just that one tooth with aligners—this patient can choose what they want to do, and I won't lose any sleep. But when providers start giving in to the whims of much younger patients, such as teenagers, just because of esthetics, that can create a treatment compromise. The cost of doing a limited correction of just a few front teeth versus a full correction of the patient's bite with braces and rubber bands may only be a 20 percent difference. That is why I want patients to know all their options.

Sometimes a parent just declines the most complex treatment; for example, they don't want to have surgery done on their child. In a case like that, we've explained the options and then must get the best result we can with the tools in our toolkit. That's not unethical, and I think that happens to every orthodontist—it's a parent's decision whether or not the child should have an elective surgery.

Sometimes, however, a parent will not want to do what is needed, and unfortunately, we will have to turn them down for treatment. For instance, if a child has an impacted canine that will not erupt in the mouth without surgical exposure, the parent may want us to just extract the tooth and then close the space, even though that is not the ideal treatment of that case. While that treatment is mechanically possible, it would leave the child without that important tooth for a lifetime. There have even been extreme instances where a parent has told us they'll just find someone else to do it, but we still won't compromise on what's best for their child.

Again, there are times when we do a compromised treatment option for an adult patient, but only after they've been properly informed and they've decided against strenuous treatment. But at the end of the day, we still know it's our job to inform each patient of their options because the impact of moving teeth creates significant changes to a person's jaw, their ability to eat, the way they look, and more—and for the long term.

Our job as orthodontists is to dissect all the information and see which of the options makes the most sense for the patient. When I go into a consult with a patient, usually I already have in mind the procedures we could use. For instance, if someone has an esthetic facial profile but their bite is off, I will want to try dental correction; I don't want to push them to go through surgery when they have ideal facial esthetics. In this instance, I would not just offer surgery as a listed option, but also offer a non-surgical option as a very viable option.

On the other hand, suppose a twenty-eight-year-old comes in with an extreme overbite, and his x-ray shows that he has an extremely narrow airway, so he likely has sleep apnea even though he is not overweight. I will do everything I can to convince this patient to move forward with the necessary surgery. I might even present that as almost a no-compromise option because the recommended surgery will positively impact their entire life, not just how they look but also how they breathe and their overall health.

Treatment Oversight

Today, we are constantly seeing patients whose jaws are in pain or who had some other adverse reaction because they tried do-it-yourself, at-home aligners. For a while, do-it-yourself aligners were a big trend: everyone thought they were great because they were cheaper and seemed easier. This treatment can really move things out of place in a bad way, so there needs to be a licensed provider with ten years of education and the experience to oversee the progress of any treatment plan.

Orthodontics is not an exact science; there's an art to it. Just like an artist halfway through a painting can't predict the exact number of hours it's going to take for that work of art to be completed, to some extent, it's the same with orthodontics. Sometimes treatment finishes earlier, sometimes later. The reason it's somewhat unpredictable from an exactness perspective is because everyone's biology is totally different, and we are constantly reassessing and redirecting treatment to achieve as close to perfect as possible. Sure, it can be frustrating for patients to not have an absolute timeline—they just want to know when the braces are coming off, as do the parents. Recently, a young patient transferred to our practice from another orthodontist. She had already been in braces for around two years, and we had her in them for another eight months. Her father wanted to know why it was taking so long, so I explained that, with us, you're never in "braces jail." We could take the braces off, but the reason we left them on was because her treatment had not yet reached the level of excellence that we deliver at our office. There was no additional cost involved; we just wanted to get her to the level of quality result that we aim for.

We never ever charge for that extra time. We consider that to be part of doing business and making sure that the patient ends up with the most ideal result. Sometimes that happens because, for instance, a tooth doesn't move like it was expected to. For instance, we may have started a patient without extracting any teeth because they were a borderline case, but then during treatment, their teeth flared forward to an unacceptable degree. What would be best for the business would be to just finish treatment and get the braces off. But because we want to deliver quality, we have to take the harder route of stopping before treatment is complete, taking new images of the teeth, and having an awkward conversation with the parents to explain why we're not happy with the progress and that we need to take out teeth to get the ideal result. Now we have to extend treatment because the plan has changed. Yet, in a case like this, we don't charge extra for that change in the treatment plan, even though it means we are providing a year or more of additional treatment for free.

Every single case, in our opinion, speaks to our reputation as a practice. That person's smile has our name on it, and so we have a certain level that we want everyone to reach, not only because we want the patient to be happy with their smile but also because they're going to be seeing and meeting people for years to come. And when they have a great smile, people will ask where they went for braces—we want them to be glad to say Sturgill Orthodontics.

A Culture of Right Decisions

Even the assistants and treatment coordinators in our practice understand how the decisions are made and what the different modalities can produce in the way of results. That's possible because we spend so much time training, which is part of the culture of the practice.

Some practices really seem to get too much into the "sell" of orthodontics. They just want to close the case, so they'll go with whatever a patient or parent wants to have done, and they stick with the same narrow line of offerings. But we think everyone's treatment should be unique, and parents and patients look to us to ethically decide which treatment is best. As I mentioned, if we think there really is only one option for a patient, we'll even tell them it's either this treatment or nothing. Our treatment coordinators see us making those kinds of decisions, and they perceive it as part of our culture. For instance, we might have a child who has not developed good dental hygiene habits and isn't ready to start braces. They may be a suitable candidate for braces and full treatment, but they're just a bit too young, and if we start them too early, it may be too much for them to handle. We'll tell the patient that we're not going to put braces on just yet, we're going to wait a few months until they learn how to brush their teeth. Our treatment coordinators see us making those kinds of ethical decisions based on what is best for the patient, not just closing the case, and those are sometimes extremely hard decisions, but they're consistently the right decisions.

Even though there are days where I think maybe I should have been a little more flexible or that it would have been easier to just move forward with treatment, I have never regretted holding that hard line. That speaks to our culture and makes for a practice that the team is always proud of. Our team members know they can trust us wholly because they see us making decisions based on what is most ideal for a patient, not what is most ideal for the business.

Clinical Corner

Be Your Consistent Best

Remember: Patients often don't know what they don't know. They may come to you concerned about a rotated front tooth but not know how to express that what they really want is a perfect smile like they saw on an actress or on Instagram. To their layman's eyes, that means just that rotated front tooth needs to be corrected. What they may not realize is that getting that perfect smile means, for example, correcting how much gum they have showing or a jaw that is set too far back.

Never underestimate the value of educating your patients; often, they don't know what can be fixed, but they just know how they look in the mirror. As the orthodontist providing treatment, don't sell your services short. You may think that a patient isn't interested in fixing more than, for instance, a rotated tooth. But with your expertise, you can help the patient have an amazing smile. Always go into the consult presenting the most ideal treatment, and you'll find that the majority of the time, patients will agree to it—they just didn't know it was an option.

 ## Practice Makes Perfect

- Patients should not be pigeonholed into the same type of treatment.
- Providers who focus solely on one type of tool may end up pushing the boundaries of that tool beyond what is best for the patient.
- Culture is about what's best for the patient, not about having bragging rights to a colleague about pushing a modality on a complex case or increasing numbers on a certain product to get recognition from a large company.
- When only one option is the best treatment for a patient, that's the only one we offer.

CHAPTER ELEVEN

Temporomandibular Joint Disorder

IT'S COMMON FOR PEOPLE to refer to the pain in their jaw as temporomandibular joint disorder (TMJ). But I often joke that telling someone you have TMJ is the same thing as saying, "I have knee" or "I have elbow." That's because TMJ is a joint—the temporomandibular joint, which is the joint connecting the jawbone to the skull. You actually have two temporomandibular joints, one on each side of the face, and they work in tandem—when one joint moves, so does the other. The TMJs are the only joints in the body that move in three directions: up and down, side to side, and forward and back.

Instead of TMJ then, the more appropriate term is TMD, which stands for temporomandibular disorder or dysfunction. But even that is not really accurate. Most people don't really have a dysfunction or disorder of the temporomandibular joint. They have more of what we would consider a facial myalgia, which is muscle-related pain, or a neuralgia, which is nerve-related pain. That pain occurs in the muscles and nerves of the TMJs.

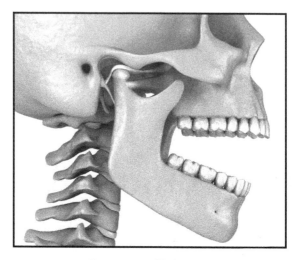

Temporomandibular Joint

People who have TMD often go through many years of failed treatments before finding solutions for their pain and problems. That's something I find very frustrating and a little bit heartbreaking when there are treatments that can bring these patients relief, and orthodontists are often key to the solutions.

Now, I'm not saying every orthodontist should treat these problems. Unfortunately, many providers shy away from treating disorders of the temporomandibular joint because they are extremely complex. A lot of providers just think their patients who complain of TMJ symptoms are neurotic, like a patient who obsesses over tiny movements in their teeth while in braces or what they perceive as a flaw with any other part of their body—their hands, their eyes, whatever.

That said, what I'm going to share with you in this chapter is not gospel either. Again, TMD is a very complex disorder, and every case is different, but we have a good road map for treatment that has been very successful for patients.

One of the reasons I first became interested in TMD was because of facial trauma my wife suffered when she was working at a veterinarian's office while we were in dental school. She was attacked by a Rottweiler, and, when she was down on the floor, the dog grabbed her lower jaw and shook her head, which caused a lot of damage to her neck and jaw. Since we were in dental school at the time, I thought I should be surrounded by the elites of doctors who could treat her jaw pain. But when I started talking to different providers, I quickly realized that no one had a clear answer and that patients were bounced from one provider to another.

My wife and I knew we would likely have patients come to us with the same problems, so while trying to find solutions for her problems, we learned an exceptional amount of information that we wanted to use to help other people. Therefore, I went on a journey to learn and read literature from people who were referred as leaders in the area a of TMJ pain and head/neck pain. That lead me from the University of Kentucky to Massachusetts General, to Johns Hopkins University—meeting program directors and reading literature.

The Pain Is Complex—and Very Real

A key to all TMD-related treatment is a proper diagnosis. Where so many providers go wrong is in trying to make TMD treatment a cookbook. It's certainly not a cookbook-type treatment. It's not like dentistry where you can find a tooth with a cavity and fix it with a filling. With TMD, there is not always an easy answer to relieving the pain. Not all patients with jaw pain can be relieved with one standard plan.

For instance, for many years, it seemed like an exponentially high number of females had TMJ pain. Many providers thought it was just because women are more vocal about pain, whereas men just don't complain. But research has found that women are actually more likely to have a physical expression of pain, especially in the head and neck region. It's also interesting that research has found that some pain receptors in the TMJ are sensitive to estrogen, which means that certain birth control medications can potentially worsen jaw pain.[9] They can also increase the likelihood of having idiopathic condylar resorption or breakdown and loss of bone in the TMJs. In fact, every patient I've seen who has had resorption issues was on birth control, and it was recommended that they stop taking it.

Regardless of the cause, I always try to comfort patients and let them know that they are not complaining. Their pain is a big deal, and it most certainly is real. They're not "crazy," and it's not uncommon for psychological stressors to have physical ramifications. For instance, it's not uncommon for patients with acute pain to be going through a divorce or have had a recent death in the family. We try to reassure them that the spike in their pain is heavily related to the stress they're going through, and it will get better.

The first step, then, is to evaluate the pain. Is it dull, achy pain? Sharp, shooting pain? How long has it been going on—did it start last week, or has it been chronic for twenty years and just recently worsened? What makes it worse: eating, cold weather, talking, singing, lying down? Is it worse when the patient first wakes up? Is the patient extremely athletic—sometimes runners can be more likely to have jaw pain. What does the patient do for a living; does it require excessive use of their jaw?

---

9   "Hormones and oral health," Cleveland Clinic, last modified June 25, 2018, accessed June 3, 2023, https://my.clevelandclinic.org/health/articles/11192-hormones-and-oral-health.

If they work at the computer all day, then their jaw pain may correlate to neck pain because of their posture while at their desk.

By understanding what is going on in their life, we can begin to diagnose the cause of the pain. With TMD, patients often know they have pain around their jaw, ear, or the side of their head. However, if we assume the pain is coming from the jaw and it's actually coming from a tooth, then we might not provide the correct treatment. By learning where the pain is coming from, we might discover that it's not jaw pain at all; it might be, for instance, trigeminal neuralgia, which is a condition that causes excruciating pain on the side of the face and is related to the trigeminal nerve pressing against a blood vessel inside the brain. Typical TMD treatments will never help with this condition; instead, the patient needs to see a neurologist to evaluate treatment options.

Misdiagnosis is not uncommon with TMD, and it's frustrating to see. For instance, I've seen patients who have been told they have trigeminal neuralgia, when they don't. One of those patients was even a physician who had been diagnosed at a large, respected hospital and, as a result, had for years been taking pain medications that came with side effects. But after talking with her, we discovered that her pain was exaggerated predictably while walking outside in chilly weather or drinking something cold, which is not typical of trigeminal neuralgia. I referred her to an endodontist to evaluate the nerve inside of a specific tooth, which was diagnosed as necrotic. All she needed was a root canal, and all of her pain went away.

Once we begin to better understand the patient's diagnosis, then it's important for them to see the right provider. After assessing patients with jaw or face pain, I may refer them to a specialist. For instance, if the likely cause of the pain is the ears, then I may refer them to an ear, nose, and throat (ENT) specialist. The key is to assess when the problem is within the scope of orthodontics and, when it is outside of that scope, help the patient get to the right provider.

Unfortunately, with TMD, sometimes there are just gray areas. We might think we know what treatment will work based on the symptoms the patient shares and on the results of various tests. If we try a treatment and it works, then we know the diagnosis was correct. But if the patient's pain does not improve, then we can rule out the first diagnosis and know that it is something else. With each step, we are upfront and fully inform the patient.

With TMD, the vast majority of patients feel their pain chiefly in the capsule (the fibrous membrane surrounding the jaw joint), or in the masseter muscle, which is a large muscle on each side of the face that helps move the mandible (lower jaw). Fewer patients present with pain that turns out to be from another source.

If the patient is diagnosed as having intracapsular pain, then we look at their bite as a potential cause. If their bite predisposes them to TMJ pain, then we want to make sure their teeth are protected with a nightguard to cushion and equilibrate the teeth during sleep. An occlusal splint, sometimes referred to as a bite plate or nightguard, is a custom-made orthotic meant to protect the teeth when a person clenches and grinds their teeth while sleeping or less commonly during daytime activities, such as driving or weightlifting.

What frustrates me is an all-too-common scenario in which patients that have been told that the only remedy for their TMJ pain is a mouthful of crowns or jaw surgery; that is almost never true. If $60,000 worth of crowns really were a solution to the problem, then using braces to move the teeth into better positions at a fraction of the cost would also fix the problem. Sometimes surgery is a solution, but that is usually for someone with a progressive disease known as condylar resorption. To date, the type of surgery that replaces the jaw with an artificial one has not been proven to predictably relieve the pain and provide the stability that one would expect. (I've seen patients who have already undergone such drastic measures and were still in significant pain.)

With us, diagnosing the problem starts by taking x-rays, which can help identify problems with the jaw. We also take an extensive medical history, perform a physical exam of the face and neck, and use an in-depth questionnaire. These measures can help us better understand the problem and begin looking at first steps to address a complex condition.

An Interdisciplinary Treatment Team

Whether we are able to provide a solution with orthodontics or relief comes from another provider, the goal is to alleviate the patient's pain. Because TMD is so difficult to accurately diagnose and treat, patients need to be sure they are completely comfortable with the treatment and provider(s).

Often, resolving TMD involves an interdisciplinary team that includes a dentist and/or orthodontist, who look at how the teeth work together and the impact that has on the bite and the jaw joint. Other professionals may include a physical therapist to help the patient strengthen their neck and back; patients who have jaw pain often have weakness in those areas. A physical therapist may recommend a standing desk and doing back exercises, both of which can make a world of difference. There may be a psychologist on the team as well, because stress is often a common factor in patients with TMD. Different individuals manifest this pathosis in myriad ways. Some feel it in their stomach and have gastrointestinal problems, others carry their stress in their neck and back, and some deal with stress by gritting their teeth, which causes a lot of jaw and facial pain. There may be a neurologist on the team because many patients who have jaw pain may also have tension-type headaches and migraines. Together, these professionals can collaborate to relieve the patient's pain.

Sometimes, however, patients compile such a team on their own. When these providers are not all in the same practice, they are not usually on the same page. As a result, the patient ends up getting different feedback—some that helps and some that does not. By the time some patients get to me, often they're feeling stuck and defeated because they've tried to find answers through so many different providers and nothing has helped, so they don't know who to believe or trust. At that point, we often become the quarterback of a team of providers who work together to provide the patient with relief.

Since we don't advertise our TMD services very much, patients usually find us through word of mouth—often a social media post from another success story. We are able to help a lot of people, but

there are also patients for whom we don't have all the answers because theirs are multidisciplinary solutions; and some problems, as an orthodontist, I can't fix. We refer patients with unique neurological syndromes to an appropriate specialist.

We also see patients whose jaw joints are locked open or closed (known as anterior disc displacement without reduction). This is one condition I believe all dentists should be trained in because it is so important that it be treated as quickly as possible. A locked jaw can cause excruciating pain and can cause lifelong loss of function if not treated right away. We had one patient who came to us after having been locked for six weeks. He had received a steroid injection from his dentist, but what was required to fully unlock the jaw was manual manipulation, which we provided that day.

Treatment Options

The TMJ is one of the most difficult joints for the body to manage because it's one of the only joints with the right and left sides connected, and its two sides must move in tandem. Think about it this way: If you hurt your right wrist, you can use your left hand and keep your right hand immobile until the wrist joint heals. But if your jaw hurts on the right side of your face, you can't use only the left side until the right side heals because you'll end up overworking the left. Because of the constant side-to-side motion of the jaw, you have to use both sides whenever you eat or swallow. You really can never completely rest one side or the other.

Another problem with the TMJ is that, when there is inflammation and swelling, there is no place for that to go. Behind the jaw is the ear (exterior auditory canal), which is a very sensitive area with a lot of nerves. In fact, patients who have jaw pain routinely say they feel like their ears are clogged or that they have water in them. Then above the jaw is the skull (articular eminence), and there is no room there for the inflammation to go superiorly. Side to side, or medially, there isn't any room for inflammation either. The TMJ is just a very tight joint with very little room compared to, say, the knee. If you injure your knee, it can swell up quite a bit because it has a lot of room for the tissue to expand. But again, since the jaw joint is such a tight space, even a little bit of swelling can cause discomfort.

When someone is clenching extremely hard all night, the jaw joint is what we call "constantly loaded," meaning it's being pressed hard up against the base of the skull, creating a lot of pressure and inflammation in the intracapsular space. That space is between what's known as the articular eminence and the condyle: the articular eminence is an area in the upper part of the temporomandibular joint that guides the jaw as it opens and closes; the condyle is the upper part of the jawbone that fits into the pocket portion of articular eminence. When the joint is not loaded, there is more room in the intracapsular space, which allows fluids to enter and escape, promoting natural healing in the TMJ area.

When a patient shows up at our office with intracapsular jaw pain, the first line of defense for this problem is to get the patient's teeth apart with some kind of nightguard (occlusal orthotic) worn during sleep. We use different types of guards depending on the patient because we don't want to make their bite worse. Our goal is to disarticulate or separate the teeth during sleep to ensure there is no occlusal interference or contact between them, which can then reduce the pressure on the jaw joint and give it a chance to heal. When the jaw is held slightly open with a nightguard, the jaw joint rests in a different position than when the teeth are clenched. Even when there is obviously a need for orthodontics to straighten someone's teeth, when there's a TMD complaint, we'll always start with some kind of removable nightguard. If that doesn't help, then we know that moving the teeth isn't going to help either because that's just changing the bite.

One treatment that has benefited a number of our patients is bio-feedback, a type of therapy that uses sensors to help a patient better understand how their body functions. Another treatment that we've found to be very helpful is botulinum toxin A (Botox), which is injected into the affected muscle. While it's long been known as a cosmetic treatment to smooth out forehead wrinkles, it also works well for TMJ pain. It works for TMD treatment because it can be injected into the masseter and temporalis muscles, which are the two muscles that do the heavy lifting of the lower jaw; injecting Botox into these muscles causes them to relax. The temporalis muscle is also the source of a lot of tension headaches for people, so relaxing that muscle helps with TMD pain and headaches. When administering it to a TMD patient, I'll have them clench while feeling the sides of their face with their fingers. Typically, they can feel their masseter muscles "pop out." That's because they've been working their jaw muscles a lot, and just like any other muscle, such as a bicep, that jaw muscle has become super strong—so strong that it's causing damage to their teeth and jaw joint. What we've seen in some facial photos over time is that the patient's jaw muscles become smaller and their face actually reshapes—instead of very square jaws, their face becomes more almond-shaped. I always joke with patients that it would be so much more helpful if, instead of our jaws, we could just train our abs to work out when we're stressed.

Some patients are a little afraid to have Botox treatment, but I prefer it over having them take an oral muscle relaxer. A small dose of an oral medication can be great for back or leg pain because those are huge muscles with a lot of blood supply, making oral medication effective. But it takes a pretty high dose of a muscle relaxer to effectively have an impact on the tiny muscles of the face. Plus, for many people, muscle relaxers just induce sleep. When we're doing an injection of Botox, we know exactly where it is going, and it's going only to the site of the problem. It's not going into the bloodstream to affect the entire body, like an oral medication does. In fact, if a patient is already seeing a neurologist who is using Botox to treat their headaches, and that treatment is being covered by insurance, then as a cost savings for the patient, I'll reach out to the neurologist to give a recommendation of Botox dosage and location to help the patient with their TMJ pain. The injection treatment also wears off in a few months, so it's not permanent like surgery, which is irreversible.

By relieving the pain, we're also relieving stress. Stress itself creates more stress, resulting in more pain. It's a cycle: pain can cause stress and stress can cause pain, a positive feedback loop that, if not stopped, results in chronic pain. Pain for more than three months is considered to be chronic pain, and that alone becomes a reason to seek help from a therapist or psychologist because living with pain is hard. Sure, there's a stigma surrounding psychology in general, but there's nothing wrong with seeing that kind of a professional. In fact, we try to comfort patients and let them know that even if there is not a lot of stress in their life, the fact that they have pain means they should be seeing someone. Chronic pain, especially in your face, is a very intimate kind of pain and something you can't escape; it's not like pain in another part of the body, such as the ankle, which feels more distant.

If you have chronic pain, please seek out professional help because, over time, it's going to be frustrating and even depressing—it can negatively change your entire outlook on life.

Clinical Corner

Seek Out Training

If you're a fellow professional, and don't feel comfortable providing more than one type of nightguard or in diagnosing when patients need to be referred to an ENT, then seek out training that is not product-based and is based on peer-reviewed literature, or come visit our office or another practice that provides these types of referrals until you are comfortable doing them yourself. That will allow you to better serve your patients.

Practice Makes Perfect

- People who have TMD often go through many years of failed treatments before finding solutions for their pain and problems.
- Evaluating and diagnosing TMJ pain start with radiographs, medical history, a physical exam of the face and neck, and an in-depth questionnaire.
- A nightguard can separate the teeth during sleep to give the jaw a chance to heal.
- Botulinum toxin A (Botox), injected into the affected muscle, can be remarkably effective in alleviating TMJ pain.
- Resolving TMD often involves an interdisciplinary team: a dentist and/or orthodontist, a physical therapist, an ENT, a psychologist, and a neurologist.
- TMD is very real and needs to be addressed because chronic pain can be frustrating and depressing and can change your entire outlook on life.

CHAPTER TWELVE

Airway Protective Orthodontics

AS AN AIRWAY PROTECTIVE orthodontics practice, Sturgill Orthodontics takes a holistic approach to working with patients. If someone's teeth fit together beautifully and they have a great smile, but they come in for an appointment and they're having a horrible day, what good have we done for them? That's why we talk to them about more than just what's going on in their mouth.

As a dentist, the first two years of professional training are identical to that of a medical doctor—we learn all the body systems. That goes a step further in orthodontic residency; we don't just look at their face and teeth; we want to look at things like whether they appear to have healthy breathing patterns or have signs/symptoms of sleep apnea or pediatric disturbed breathing.

We sometimes have patients come to us because their bite doesn't seem to fit anymore, and they have a lot of space in their lower teeth. Well, it's not normal in your fifties to just have a lot of space open up between your teeth; teeth often crowd over time, but they don't typically develop space. When we see that, we start thinking about the airway being the problem because the tongue is fighting to open the airway every night, and it's thrusting forward, pushing the teeth out of place. We've even seen patients who had the space closed up with orthodontics from another provider, but then the space opened back up again. Again, that's because the tongue is fighting for the airway. Your body is basically doing all it can at night to keep your airway open. We usually send these patients for a sleep study. Even though it takes extra effort to form relationships with sleep centers and we're not paid for that, we still see it as part of the job as an orthodontics provider and the quarterback in treating patients with problems outside our expertise.

A sleep study can help determine how much a person's sleep is disrupted by their airway periodically closing up, causing them to consciously or unconsciously wake up to keep breathing. Often, the sleep study will determine that these patients are ideal candidates for a continuous positive airway pressure (CPAP), the gold standard in helping patients with sleep apnea. After they're fitted for a CPAP, they'll start sleeping better and feeling better, and then they will still come back to us to have the spaces in their teeth closed—and this time they will stay closed because their tongue is no longer fighting them for an airway.

For those patients who need but cannot tolerate a CPAP or custom-fabricated sleep appliance (both of which I'll discuss later in this chapter), there are some other surgical options with varying success rates; many have had low success rates over a long period of time, and they can be very painful. One is known as a uvulopalatopharyngoplasty (UPPP), which involves resecting the uvula, soft palate, and tonsil tissues of the throat to increase the oropharyngeal airspace or the airway in the throat.[10] Another relatively new treatment involves an implant that stimulates the airway muscles during sleep to keep the airway open. These options, in my opinion, are better than nothing but should not be the first thing that people jump at as a solution because, again, the CPAP is really the gold standard for sleep apnea. The surgical option that has shown the best results for treatment of sleep apnea is maxillomandibular advancement (MMA), which I'll discuss later in the chapter.[11]

Diagnosis and Treatment— the Earlier the Better

Parents often don't equate orthodontics to the airway, but the first thing we do when we see really young patients ages seven to sixteen is to take a lateral cephalogram x-ray to look at the child's airway. We look at the adenoids and tonsils because it's very common for kids to have enlargement or inflammation in those tissues. When we see that, we'll also start looking at other parts of the medical history. Do they wake up tired? Do they snore at night? Do they have dark circles under their eyes? Do they still wet the bed or have attention deficit hyperactivity disorder (ADHD)? All of those things can point to what is known as pediatric disturbed breathing or pediatric sleep apnea.

---

10 Akram Khan, Kannan Ramar, Supriya Maddirala, Oren Friedman, John F. Pallanch, and Eric J. Olson, "Uvulopalatopharyngoplasty in the Management of Obstructive Sleep Apnea: The Mayo Clinic Experience," *Mayo Clinic Proceedings* 84, no. 9 (September 2009): 795–800, https://www.ncbi.nlm.nih.gov/pmc/articles/PMC2735429/.

11 C. R. John, S. Gandhi, A. R. Sakharia, and T. T. James, T. T., "Maxillomandibular Advancement Is a Successful Treatment for Obstructive Sleep Apnoea: A Systematic Review and Meta-analysis," *International Journal of Oral and Maxillofacial Surgery* 47, no. 12 (2018): 1561–1571, https://doi.org/10.1016/j.ijom.2018.05.015.

When we see those kinds of symptoms, we make the referral to an ENT, and we send the x-ray along to that consult to help that ENT decide whether to perform an adenoidectomy and/or tonsillectomy on the child. We don't bill for that assessment and referral, and we often have parents come back and thank us for catching the problem: "My kid is like a new kid!" they'll tell us. "They're sleeping through the night, they don't get sick as often, they're happier."

If a person can't breathe through their nose while they are asleep, they'll have to breathe through their mouth. When you breathe through your mouth, your tongue rests in the lower jaw instead of in the roof of the mouth, where it should naturally rest. Your tongue resting in the roof of your mouth is what makes your maxilla, or upper jaw, wider, and that development occurs during childhood. A wider maxilla results in a better airway, because the roof of the mouth is connected to the nasal passages. Unfortunately, we often see patients at a young age have a really narrow upper jaw.

Typically, two things cause a narrow upper jaw. One is a thumb-sucking habit, which pushes upward on the upper jaw. All that pushing causes the upper jaw to form around that thumb's upward pressure. The other is obligate mouth breathing, which means the person is obligated to breathe through their mouth while sleeping. This typically occurs because of some obstruction of the airway, either in the nasopharynx or the nasal cavity. When this happens, instead of the tongue resting in its natural position in the upper jaw, where it helps to create a wider maxilla, it rests in the lower jaw. As a result, the upper jaw then narrows from all the pressure placed on it by the lips and cheeks.

There's a lot of great literature that shows that expanding the upper jaw, the maxilla, increases nasal airway volume and nasal airway passages by as much as twofold—a pretty big improvement.[12] When we find out a child is not sleeping well, meaning they likely have pediatric disturbed breathing or pediatric sleep apnea, we first find out whether their tonsils and adenoids need to be removed. We also often use an expander appliance to widen their maxilla, which makes more space in the roof of their mouth for their tongue to reside, opens the nasal airway so that they can breathe through their nose, and restores the maxilla to the appropriate size. That can really be life-changing for a child and the parent; it's one of my favorite treatments we offer because it can have a really big impact on the whole family. Instead of having to constantly deal with illnesses and the effects of a child who isn't sleeping well, we can make such a big difference by opening the child's airway so that they breathe while they sleep. That's the primary way we provide treatment as an airway protective orthodontist.

The second way we provide airway protective orthodontics is by looking at ways to move the jaws and correct the bite. If there is an option to move one of the jaws forward, either the upper or lower, we almost always go with that option versus moving a jaw backward to meet a jaw that has retruded (retrognathic).

Historically, when one jaw is in a correct position and one is retrusive or set back farther, the preferred treatment was to retrude the other jaw—retract it to meet the jaw that was malpositioned. These days, whenever it's possible to do so, we typically take the approach of trying to bring the affected jaw forward to meet the other jaw that's already more forward and in a better position. That's because moving some structures forward tends to bring all the structures forward, and that tends to be airway protective in the long term, even in a

---

12   Ela Hakan and Juan Martin Palomob, "Three-Dimensional Evaluation of Upper Airway Following Rapid Maxillary Expansion: A CBCT Study," *Angle Orthodontist* 84, no 2 (2014): 265–273, https://doi.org/10.2319/012313-71.1.

patient who does not have sleep disorder or sleep apnea. For instance, a sixteen-year-old is going to be sixty-six one day, so we want to be as protective as possible of their airway for the long term.

A third way we address airway is surgically. We address the airway during orthognathic surgery; otherwise it can be negatively impacted. This surgery is used to reposition the jaws, so we want to make sure that the result is jaws and airway in the ideal position when the surgery is done. Sometimes, we recommend orthognathic surgery when a patient has a very narrow airway because their lower jaw is so retrusive. These are patients who have typically normal body mass index (BMI) but who still suffer from sleep apnea (overweight can be a factor in sleep apnea). In these patients, their very retrognathic lower jaw has allowed the throat musculature to collapse, which anatomically creates a smaller airway. We send these patients out for a sleep study, and if it turns out they have sleep apnea, the good news is that their airway can be fixed permanently with surgery, which insurance will usually pay for. Plus, their face will look better, and their bite will function better—for these patients, the surgery is a win all the way around.

We also have patients come to us who have already been diagnosed with sleep apnea, and they have done enough research online to know that one of the ways to correct it is with jaw surgery. In these cases, the surgery, which is known as maxillary mandibular advancement (MMA), actually moves both jaws forward to open the airway. This treatment is one where a patient can essentially permanently correct obstructive sleep apnea.

Finally, we address airway using sleep appliances. Sleep appliances work by positioning the lower jaw forward, which helps open the airway. These appliances are fabricated to custom fit the patient's mouth, and they are worn during sleep. These are typically made for patients for whom we don't do orthodontic treatment, but these patients show up because they have sleep apnea, they've done the research, and they know that they can wear an appliance in their mouth during sleep instead of using a CPAP machine. While CPAP is the gold standard, some patients cannot tolerate the device. It's bulky and sometimes uncomfortable to wear, it's hard to travel with, and it makes people feel claustrophobic—some people just don't like to wear it. Plus, sleep appliances are more convenient when traveling or going camping and there is no electric outlet to power the CPAP appliance.

Sleep appliances can produce orthodontic side effects because they pull the jaw forward slightly, which is actually an unnatural position. At some point, it's going to feel like your teeth don't fit anymore because after years of sleep appliance use, the teeth will shift a little, no matter how good an appliance it is and how well it's made. It's important to set expectations with these appliances, but they provide real benefit for a lot of people who need their sleep disorder addressed.

Clinical Corner
The Truth Is in the Middle

When it comes to airway protective orthodontics, there can be extremes. There are those who say that orthodontics is going to change someone's airway tremendously; on the other side, there's the belief that nothing orthodontically impacts the airway. We believe the truth lies somewhere in the middle, and we use our expertise to provide those treatments that will help a patient while referring other patients out to the best providers for other treatments that can resolve their issues.

Practice Makes Perfect

- An airway protective orthodontics practice takes a holistic approach to working with patients.
- Dental training begins with two years of medical training, giving us insight into all the systems of the body.
- Airway protective orthodontics is about helping each patient beyond just face and teeth; it's about helping them have a better life.
- With children, a lateral cephalogram x-ray can look at the airway and see whether adenoids are enlarged.
- In children, expanding the upper jaw, the maxilla, increases nasal airway volume and nasal airway passages by as much as twofold.[13]
- Another way we address the airway is by moving retrusive jaws forward, through orthognathic surgery or MMA surgery, or by custom-fabricating sleep appliances.

---

13   Ibid.

CHAPTER THIRTEEN

The Value of Treatment

RECENTLY, THE FATHER OF one of our young patients was frustrated because his child's treatment was going to take a little longer to complete, and he thought that meant it was going to cost more than he was originally quoted. He thought he was going to have to keep paying more for the remaining months that his child was in treatment. But that's not the way it works here. While we try to guess accurately on the timeline, if we're wrong, it's on us. If we need to see the patient for ten or thirty more appointments after the payments are complete, that's not profitable for us, but we're going to do it because the culture in our office is to work toward achieving clinical excellence. We're not looking at whether each case is profitable; we're just looking at the individual case. And when they're done, they're done. In fact, we make a point to have these areas of the practice separated—

the doctors just treat the case, and our financial department handles everything else. Some parents are surprised when they start to ask me or another doctor a financial question, and we have to quickly explain we sincerely aren't aware and direct them to our financial coordinator. We do this intentionally, allowing the orthodontist to walk into every case and simply do what is best for that patient.

One of the questions I'm often asked is why treatment is so expensive. There are myriad avenues we could follow to try to answer that question. Ultimately, treatment isn't as expensive as it might be if it weren't for the efficiencies developed over time. These include technologies that have kept the price of orthodontics reasonable compared to inflation and the cost of braces in the past. In fact, compared to treatment in the 1940s and 1950s, it's actually lower cost today because technology has allowed for so many efficiencies.

Obviously, it's still a substantial investment for families. But it's a different kind of investment compared to other types of treatments. For instance, a laser procedure on the eye comes with a one-time cost of several thousand dollars for a single procedure (appointment). What are you paying for when you go to the ophthalmologist for that eye surgery? You're paying for the years of education and knowledge and skill that the provider has to correct a problem with your vision, as well as the cost involved to produce the remarkable technology to perform such a procedure along with the associated staff to support the procedure. With orthodontic treatment, you're paying for the eleven years of school your provider went through to gain the knowledge and skill of correcting your smile in a way that provides long-term health and function of your teeth, face, and jaws. Plus, orthodontic treatment is typically provided over a two-year period. When you break down the cost of treatment over that period of time, it isn't nearly as expensive as it may seem by having a lump sum for a one-time treatment.

Another factor to consider is that, at Sturgill Orthodontics, treatment is all-inclusive. It includes all of the appointments, even if you go beyond your treatment time or need something extra. When you take into consideration all of these points, then it becomes clear that there should be an appropriate fee attached to the treatment.

At Sturgill Orthodontics, there's a range of costs for treatment, from $1,000 to $10,000; the cost is unique to every single patient and their specific treatment plan. While it might be easier and more profitable for us to charge a single fee and fix everyone's teeth the same way, we customize every treatment plan to the needs of the patient. In addition, we often tell patients which option is the best bang for their buck. For example, instead of paying money to just align their teeth, we may suggest a more complex treatment, such as a tooth replacement or extraction. Even though the orthodontic fee would be the same, suggesting the more complex treatment is something the patient may not want to hear because it's more than that simple alignment they wanted. But we want patients to know what we're doing, why we're doing it, and what they're getting for their dollar.

A common misunderstanding is that the hardware is very expensive, but it only makes up about 25 percent of the total cost of treatment. People often think that the braces are the most expensive part of treatment, and I've even had patients go to a provider outside of the United States to get braces put on and then come to us to finish treatment, thinking that it will cost less. It doesn't work like that. While the brackets used in braces are part of the toolkit, ultimately, they are just little handles placed on each tooth. Treatment is more about our expertise in managing the movement of the teeth. When people have a tool put on by another provider, it's not a set-it-and-forget-it situation—the braces don't just magically move teeth on their own. In that situation, we end up taking off the braces put on by the other provider and replace them with tools that we can use, and then we manage the movement of the teeth over a period of a couple of years. At every one of our appointments, there are licensed providers and assistants overseeing care.

With orthodontics, once you're a patient, you're a patient for life. Some of the fee for orthodontics means that you're now under the orthodontist's care. That doesn't mean everything is going to be free forever. For instance, if you have a problem with a retainer, there's a nominal fee to fix it. But the cost of braces is almost like a membership to the practice because now you are a patient of record, and we're going to take care of all your orthodontic needs.

When you think about all that goes into treatment, the cost becomes a lot more digestible. It's not like a single event, such as Lasik eye surgery. Orthodontics is not one and done; you're really paying for care over a long period of time.

Orthodontics can even save you money on dentistry in the long run because having teeth that fit together well can prevent or reduce damage from improper wear that can be difficult for the dentist to repair. When teeth are in the wrong position, they are set up to damage one another. It's impossible to know who will be impacted by that. All we know is, if teeth fit incorrectly, then you are set up for the potential of that damage. We've seen fifteen-year-olds who have already significantly worn their teeth down. If they don't have orthodontic work done, then by the time they are twenty-five, they will need significant dental work, such as crowns, just to regain their function. On the flip side, we've seen people in their sixties whose bite doesn't fit well, but there is little to no wear. All we know is if the teeth fit incorrectly, there is the risk for crowding and wear. Crowded teeth are harder to clean, and depending on the crowding, it can be really hard for the dentist to repair decay. So, orthodontics impacts not only dental work that you need now but also dental work that you may need in the future. If your bite fits appropriately, and your teeth are appropriately aligned, then your dental work is more predictable, and it is likely going to look better and last longer. Considering that dental insurance doesn't always cover some kinds of repairs, orthodontics can also present a cost savings by reducing damage to teeth.

Beyond the monetary value, there's also the non-cash value. A bite that's off or crowded teeth only worsen with age. If you are not happy with your smile now, you won't be happy with it later. Later correction will be harder, take longer, and cost more to correct.

In chapter 9, I also talked about how people with straight teeth are perceived to be smarter and are more likely to land a job. That's just a truth of the bias of the world we live in. We see firsthand the impact of straight teeth on patients who are very shy, timid, or less likely to smile—not only young patients and teens but also adults. Over the course of the two years, we see them start to feel more confident and become more outgoing. With children, we see them engaging more with others and taking part in new activities. With adults, we often see them pursuing a different career, going back to school, changing their hairstyle, going to the gym, and even losing weight. It kind of sparks patients' self-esteem to have straighter teeth, and it's really hard to put a dollar figure on the value of that.

Do You Have to Wear a Retainer?

Orthodontics can be a singular investment; you shouldn't need ongoing active orthodontic treatment as long as your orthodontist did a good job setting you up with retainers and you do a good job wearing them. If retention is done correctly, orthodontics is typically a once-in-a-lifetime investment. It's not like a teeth cleaning, where you have to go in every six months for another one.

Similar to how we are with treatment modalities, at Sturgill Orthodontics, our retainer protocol is completely customizable because every case is truly unique. We provide a variety of removable retainers, such as clear Essix-style retainers, Hawley retainers, wire and acrylic retainers, and bonded or permanent retainers. The bonded or permanent retainer is a little wire that is adhered to the back of the front teeth. These are not actually "permanent," such as a tattoo; we can remove them at any time; the patient just cannot take them in and out.

The majority of patients will use either an Essix or a Hawley-style removable retainer. Some patients get to choose between two based on comfort or preference of style. Still others must use the retainers we recommend because of their particular case. Which retainers are used depends on several factors, including where the patient's teeth started out—were they spaced, rotated, impacted—and knowing which movements have a really high chance of relapsing or moving back into their original positions. If there's a really high chance of relapse, we'll lean toward using the permanent retainer combined with a removable retainer. We can't use a permanent retainer on every single tooth, so we provide a removable retainer for the back teeth to ensure everything is secured. If the patient had surgery on their upper jaw, we're not going to put them in a flexible, clear retainer. We're going to put them in an acrylic retainer or a thick nightguard because surgical movement has a tendency to want to relapse. Depending on the case, we may put a bite plate on their retainer because they have a tendency toward a deep bite. Or we may put them in a nightguard as their final retainer because they grind their teeth.

We don't have a singular protocol, which can make for complexities when running an office that treats thousands of patients. Sure, the best business decision would be for us to offer the same retainer for every patient. Instead, we have a unique treatment plan for every single patient, and that includes specific retainers.

We also offer retainer insurance covering two retainers per year with a copay of around $25. That's a valuable option for someone who is really planning to keep their teeth in great shape. Without the insurance, replacement of a single retainer costs almost $300. For around $1,000, you can replace grungy or lost retainers a couple times a year for ten years, making it a great investment for teenagers who always manage to lose their retainer but never their phone.

The Value of the Predictability

I am confident that the level of care provided by my team is as good or better than any practice in the entire country because we have a team that strives for excellence and truly cares about our patients. What that means from a value perspective is, for instance, if you're a mom and you go somewhere else where the prices are very competitive, you may want to choose that practice to save a few hundred dollars. I get it. It's not always the case that treatment costs more at Sturgill; in fact, sometimes it costs less here. But I get it if you're trying to save a few hundred dollars.

Remember, what you're paying for is not only excellence in treatment. You're also paying for communication handled with grace and confidence, good service, a kinder culture, and all the things that make orthodontics a more pleasant experience. What many people don't realize is that it costs money to create a good culture; it's an investment in our business when we have to set aside time just to do things to build our culture. Staff meetings, team-building events, continuing education—all these things are investments that the practice has to make to keep our standard high and to keep our culture where it needs to be.

In short, what you're paying for as a parent or a patient is quality and predictability: you know you can come to our office and you will be welcomed with a warm drink and a comfortable place to sit with your computer while you wait. You're paying for the good feeling that you have when you come to the practice. This is not a place you're going to dread coming to, or where you will be treated rudely, or leave in a state of confusion. It's a place where you know you're going to be in good, capable, caring hands.

Clinical Corner

What Is Your Value?

Do you, as a provider, feel confident in the product that you are providing? Do you feel confident in the skill of your team? Your answers to these questions can help you determine your value. Once you have that confidence, don't sell yourself short. If you can provide excellence, then create an office and a system where you can show patients how you're different and how you provide excellence. If you don't know how to do that, then reach out to me or another practice that knows how. We can show you how we do it every day.

Practice Makes Perfect

- Technologies have introduced efficiencies into orthodontics that have allowed treatment to remain reasonably priced compared to how much braces used to cost.
- Treatment is typically provided over a two-year period, which makes it easier for many families to cover the cost and makes it seem less expensive on the front end.
- When paying for orthodontics, you're paying for expertise and all the elements that make for a pleasant and predictable experience.
- Treatment at Sturgill Orthodontics is all-inclusive.
- With orthodontics, once you're a patient, you're a patient for life.
- If retention is done correctly, orthodontics is typically a once-in-a-lifetime investment.

CHAPTER FOURTEEN

Are All Orthodontists the Same?

MANY OTHER AREAS OF HEALTHCARE have become commoditized, and that works for some of them. But it really doesn't work well in orthodontics. The problem is people don't understand that orthodontics is not a commodity. Without this understanding, the only differentiator becomes price.

Let's say you're out shopping for a car. That brand-new car is identical at three different dealerships, so all you're really shopping for is the best price because you're getting the same product. But there is a difference in treatment between orthodontists.

I even have close friends who will go to a dentist who, I'll tell them, is not top on my list of providers that I would see. But when I ask why they are going there, the response is: "Well, my insurance covers it." They think all dentists have the same level of skill and technology and treatment. But there are huge differences in all of those elements.

It's the same with orthodontics. As an orthodontist, I can sometimes see a smile and tell whose work it is because orthodontists often have certain elements as artistic staples. That's one of the things that makes orthodontics unique—a significant part of it is art. That's unlike treatment through a primary care physician, where art isn't necessarily one of the things on the table. For instance, if someone tells you they had lab work done, you're not going to be able to determine by the results who their primary care provider was. So, while a lot of orthodontics is science-based, there is an artistic piece as well as the provider's particular philosophical approach to treatment.

While everyone may have their own unique goals or attributes or dogma for life, one of the things that the orthodontists at Sturgill Orthodontics do when deciding on patient treatment is to pause and ask ourselves questions such as, "What if this were my daughter? What would be my treatment decision?" Or to take it even a step further, Dr. Williams says she asks herself chairside, "What if I was treating Jesus? How would I treat this patient if they were Jesus?" We really try to put pause in our days to not forget that the person in front of us is someone's daughter or son, mom or dad. This is someone who matters the world to someone else. This way we don't feel like we're running around the clinic just treating mouths that have teeth.

It's truly humbling to realize that the teeth I'm working on are attached to a mouth that's attached to a body that's attached to a soul that's attached to a community. It's unbelievably humbling that, where I come from, now thousands of people trust me to serve their family. That is an honor I rise to every day.

I remember what it was like when my parents took me to an orthodontist as a kid, and they didn't have the right questions to ask.

They didn't know good treatment from bad treatment. They were just doing the best they could for their kid, sacrificially paying for orthodontics probably over their own basic dental care needs because, like every parent, they wanted to give their child the best. I remember those experiences when I now work with parents who come in and are trusting me to do the right thing. They are working hard for the money that they're passing over to me to take good care of their child. By always reminding myself of that, this is no longer just a business, and patients are not just teeth. That mindset continually keeps me humble and makes me continually strive for excellence. How can we make the treatment better? How can we make the customer experience better? How can we make sure that every parent and patient is getting the best value for their investment?

That's why, when I'm asked, "Are all orthodontists the same?" I answer no, and neither are all practices. There's going to be a different feel, and they're not all the same, because they don't all have the same treatments or culture. They don't all use the same technologies. They don't all have the same training. They don't all have the same philosophies. That's why it's important to do your due diligence. If you go to a provider who uses only a one-off, singular appliance, that should be alarming.

For instance, as I write this book, some providers are in trouble for disastrous results when using an appliance they said could grow the maxilla, or the upper jaw. In youth, we have appliances that can widen the maxilla, but there is no way to grow the front of the maxilla as an adult. The only thing the problem appliance did was move the teeth out of the bone. The provider got in trouble because he's not fully trained and because there is no single dogma that should be believed wholeheartedly as a treatment philosophy. Unfortunately, this provider's treatment was only brought to the attention in the news after several patients lost their front teeth.

That's one of the things Sturgill Orthodontics does really well; we do not subscribe to a single philosophy. There are core principles that we really try to go by: we do treatment that is airway protective, moves the teeth into a better position for lip support, and helps improve the smile, and we try not to extract unless we have to. But ultimately, we look at every single person biologically to see what treatment will work well for them for the long term. You will never hear from myself or any provider who works at Sturgill Orthodontics a blanket statement such as "I can treat every person without extraction," "I can grow bone on adults," or "I can modify the jaw of an adult without surgery." We are not so bold as to assume everyone's biology is the same, nor does everyone have the same teeth. Some patients have thin gums, short roots, and a small bone housing. When that's the case, we're not going to be able to move their teeth very far without sacrificing the integrity of their teeth. That's different from someone who has thick gums, long roots, and large amounts of bone; with this patient, we can probably get some pretty significant movement without risking the health of their teeth.

Again, orthodontics is not a commodity. It's a doctor who's looking at you and diagnosing your teeth or your child's teeth to determine how much and what kind of movement is possible without damaging their health. If someone comes in with a history of severe jaw pain and clicking and locking, they're in a very fragile state, and we're not going to immediately start aggressive treatment on them, like surgery. Instead, we will start off with treatment that we know will not worsen their pain. If an adult patient has a very severe malocclusion that requires surgery to correct, but they decline surgery, we will instead do a creative nonsurgical treatment plan, which actually might be a more difficult option. We opt for that treatment plan because we are always game for the Hail Mary as long as that particular patient's dentoalveolar complex is healthy enough to move forward with treatment.

But we're also not afraid to tell a patient after an exam that they're just not a good candidate for orthodontics if they're not willing to do surgery when it's needed. Either surgery or nothing, we might say, even knowing that someone down the street might be willing to put braces on them. We can do that too, but the end result would not put them in a better position. Therefore, unless we can look at someone and wholeheartedly say we can take them to a better place, then we are not even going to offer to take them on that trip.

Clinical Corner

Remember

Remember why you got into this. You know it's not about the quantity. It's about the quality. That's why you became an orthodontist in the first place. One of the things that drives a lot of people to be a specialist is the desire to be excellent in one area and not feel like you're just good at several things. I know that's what drove me into orthodontics as a profession. You worked your tail off getting into and making it through a residency program, so don't come out of it and decide that you know enough and now it's time to just focus on making money. Remember that your patients are the best examples of what you worked so hard to achieve, but there are people behind those smiles—people who truly matter to someone else.

Practice Makes Perfect

- Orthodontics is not a commodity.
- There is an art to orthodontics, and orthodontists tend to have staple artistic touches in their work.
- All orthodontists are not alike: they don't offer the same treatments or technologies, and they don't have the same training or philosophies.
- It's important to do your due diligence when looking for a provider.

A Final Note to Patients and Parents

AS A PATIENT OR PARENT, if you go to a dental practice that has a new dentist every time you go for a cleaning, that might not be the best practice. That's not saying there is anything wrong with turnover; we have that ourselves because people relocate. But if you go to a provider and every time the entire staff is new and the entire office is like a revolving door, that should be a red flag that something isn't harmonious. There is a reason people don't feel good about working there, and it might be a sign that you need to find a different provider.

When you're searching for a provider, don't let a small factor be the decision-maker. Look at the bigger picture of which provider had a culture that made you feel confident that they will do everything they can to make sure that your child or you have the best result possible. Ultimately, the orthodontist's conviction toward being a good provider and having a well-trained team that is excited to help you get a great result will drive better care, and you'll be so much happier with your results.

Hopefully you have found something educational about ortho-dontics and/or inspirational to office culture that helps you in your office/practice or helps you in deciding what orthodontist to see for your children. If something you read in this book invigorates and excites you and you want to entrust *our* practice to care for you or for your child, then please reach out to Sturgill Orthodontics at https:// sturgillorthodontics.com/.